Gerard Manley Hopkins

THE POET AS VICTORIAN

Gerard Manley Hopkins

THE POET AS VICTORIAN

Wendell Stacy Johnson

Cornell University Press
ITHACA, NEW YORK

To Amos V. Johnson
and Vera E. Johnson

Preface

This study of the poetry of Hopkins represents the converging of several interests. It is one result of a year's work on Victorian art and literature supported by a fellowship from the John Simon Guggenheim Memorial Foundation. What was to have been an essay or possibly a chapter relating the landscape imagery of Hopkins to his early interest in Pre-Raphaelitism and to the possible influence of John Ruskin exceeded its original bounds and gradually took on a new character. It became a series of explications and comments emphasizing the relation of the poet to his Victorian culture, literary as well as artistic. In effect, the work began to express my interest in Hopkins as a Victorian poet, a poet to be compared with Tennyson, Browning, Arnold, and Swinburne.

Although no extended studies have given primary emphasis to Hopkins as a Victorian, a number of critics have recognized the importance of his age to his work. These include Arthur Mizener, in the Kenyon Critics volume of 1949, W. H. Gardner, in his indispensable two-volume study, and Elizabeth Schneider, in several recent essays; I am indebted to them as well as to various other scholars cited in my notes. The fourth edition of the *Poems* of Gerard Manley Hopkins (1967), edited by W. H. Gardner and Norman H. Mackenzie, is my source for all passages of poetry, which are quoted by permission of Oxford University Press.

Part of my first chapter was delivered as a paper at the 1962 meeting of the Modern Language Association and was published in the *Victorian Newsletter* of Spring, 1962.

Finally, I take pleasure in acknowledging generous aid from a number of mentors, colleagues, and friends, and in thanking, for his encouragement, Professor Gordon N. Ray, President of the Guggenheim Foundation; for his gift of Hopkins material, Dr. Kurt Mitchells of London; for his help with the typescript, Professor Gerald M. Pinciss of Hunter College, The City University of New York; and for their close reading and most helpful criticism, Professor Allan Danzig of City College, The City University of New York, and Professor Park Honan of Brown University.

W. S. J.

Hunter College
The City University of New York
March 1968

Contents

Gerard Manley Hopkins

THE POET AS VICTORIAN

Introduction:
Fifty Years After

In 1918 Robert Bridges published the poems of Gerard Manley Hopkins, only a handful of which had
previously appeared. Since then, the influence of Hopkins upon other poets has been significant, and criticism
has been increasingly devoted to him. This criticism
includes numerous explications of one lyric, "The
Windhover," and several essays on the body of the
verse emphasizing such special matters as the poet's
prosodic practice—to which he himself gave new ter-
minology—and his use of the key terms *inscape* and
instress. The importance of rhythm and sound in Hopkins can hardly be exaggerated and should never be
overlooked: verbal echoes, oddities of stress, and shifts
in rhythmic pattern constitute the shape, or *scape*, of
each poem which is the embodiment of its meaning.
And the words *inscape* and *instress*, with their theological implications, are crucial. But restating prosodic

theory and narrowly defining these terms do not necessarily amount to a critical reading of Hopkins' poetry. In fact, Hopkins makes his "sprung rhythm," based on the number of stressed (and frequently alliterated) syllables rather than on the conventional syllabic-metrical line, sound more complicated than it has to be for a reading of the verse. His love of fine distinctions serves in his prose to make such a word as *inscape* seem more philosophically precise than it always is in lines of his poetry. Its sense of the peculiar inner nature of things and persons, expressed in form and gesture, is enough to go on. It is less important to establish as a general proposition whether or not the word is to be distinguished from *pitch*, personal intensity, or even from the sheer selfhood of the immortal soul, than to see how the word works in a poem. Like other poets, Hopkins uses words not as invariably defined logical counters but as interacting elements in a complex of sense.

To read Hopkins with intelligent and sensitive university students—particularly those who lack a religious background—is to realize how much the poetry needs and deserves explication, but explication that includes some awareness of context. The context of Hopkins' art is not only religious. He is a Christian poet, a poet of nature, and a Victorian poet. The last point has been made least often and least well.

Is man, the creature who turns his attention inward to himself, in harmony with the external order or alienated from it? In one form or another, this question haunts Victorian literature. It confronts Tennyson, Arnold, Swinburne, and, to a lesser extent, Browning. My intention is to consider Hopkins as a Victorian poet, as a poet who is confronted by this post-Romantic problem. It is a question of understanding the self in an intensely self-conscious age and especially of relating the idea of the self to the idea of nature—to the idea of the physical universe that may or may not be in essence a spiritual or moral universe. It is a question to which Hopkins' mind is addressed in a series of poems that evoke a variety of natural images, images of the sea, of the bird, of seasonal vegetation, and of fire and light.

Each of four centrally important poems uses such imagery to explore the relation of self to nature: *The Wreck of the Deutschland*, which is in part about the natural destructive force of the ocean; "The Windhover," which first pictures and then reflects upon the flight of a bird; "Spring and Fall," which relates autumnal foliage to human mortality; and the late lines "That Nature is a Heraclitean Fire, and of the Comfort of the Resurrection," which assert human immortality by shifting from a natural imagery of brilliant light to a metaphorical imagery of transcendent light. The first of these opposes active nature to the self, the second makes a parallel between active nature and the self, the third makes a parallel between passive nature and the self, and the last opposes passive nature to a "Jackself" that is virtually transfigured.

In comparing these poems to others by Hopkins that

use similar imagery and in explicating them from this thematic point of view, one can touch only lightly on a number of important topics—on prosody, on theology, on biography. But the following chapters, while concentrating upon individual poems, are meant to suggest how consistently Hopkins's poetry expresses Victorian preoccupations, how directly he attacks the problems raised in so much of Victorian literature, and how remarkable his success is. Some fifty years after the first volume of his work appeared, it can be claimed that Hopkins is much more than a technician or a versifying intellectual priest, that in fact he belongs, with Tennyson, Browning, and Arnold, to the highest rank of the Victorian poets.

1 Hopkins in His Times

Gerard Manley Hopkins was born in 1844 and died in 1889. Chronologically, then, he is a Victorian. Yet when Arthur Mizener writes of him, sixty years after his death, as "Victorian Hopkins," the title may seem to many readers perverse.[1] The essay so entitled does not deal at length with Hopkins' major interests and only suggests that these are essentially Victorian, that the poet has much in common with such contemporaries as Tennyson and Arnold, and of course Ruskin and Newman. The value of the essay lies in Mizener's stating at least what many earlier twentieth-century critics have denied. Sometimes Hopkins has not been recognized as a Victorian poet because most of his verse was not published until 1918; because some of his poetic techniques are so individual that they seem eccentric and atypical of any period; and because his influence on modern poets—Auden, for example—has made him appear, in retrospect, to have been born before his time.

[1] See *Gerard Manley Hopkins*, by the Kenyon Critics (London, 1949), pp. 95–112.

Does he really belong to any period? In certain ways, every writer is necessarily a part of the world that produces him. Hopkins' "Victorianism" is hard to define, however, not only because he is deliberately peculiar, but also because he springs from an age of peculiar writers, an age full of variety and contradiction. In order truly to understand what it can mean to say that Hopkins is a Victorian, we shall have to understand the general characteristics, if any, of Victorian literature. No age in cultural history has been more blandly or more foolishly defined: "Victorian" can mean smug or prudish or imperialistic or hypocritical or over-optimistic, any or all of these. In fact, no age in English history is more difficult to define fairly.

Among the difficulties—for example, setting time limits to the period and deciding whether to describe the temper of a nation or only the qualities of its more permanent literature—perhaps the most serious, because the least obvious, is that of realizing our own vantage point; of understanding just how close to us Victorian writers and intellectuals are as compared with their Romantic predecessors, and just how distant from us they are as well. We may smile at the very young who foreshorten centuries to characterize as Victorian almost any writer who lived before 1900. But at the same time we can easily ignore the nearer perspective and choose to see only the strikingly modern ideas in Arnold, Newman, and George Eliot—or the modern quality in Hopkins. Instead, we should dis-

tinguish Victorianism from both what came before
and what came after it, if we agree that there is such a
thing, and if we sense, as did many Victorians after
1850, a paradoxical unity in that vertiginously changing
period of fifty or sixty years.[2]

By now, at least, we should know upon what lines
our generalizing cannot be done. As a number of scholars have observed, no single idea, world picture, or

[2] Early in the period, a feeling that there was some "Spirit
of the Age" challenged Carlyle as well as John Stuart Mill to
define it. The problem of defining those times now challenges
us again to characterize "Victorianism," this "spirit of the
age." These very phrases are, in fact, the titles of first chapters
in the two most interesting recent books on the Victorian mind,
Jerome H. Buckley's *The Victorian Temper* (Cambridge,
Mass., 1951), and Walter Houghton's *The Victorian Frame of
Mind* (New Haven, 1957). Both Buckley and Houghton are
aware how difficult the task is, how many elements there are
that constitute this age and how contradictory they are. Perhaps, a year before the great reform bill and six years before
Victoria's reign began, Carlyle and the young Mill were less
aware of all such contradictions, real and potential. But for the
mid-Victorians these had already become evident. Here, for
example, is the *Athenaeum* reviewer of Ruskin's *Pre-Raphaelitism*, writing in 1851: "Whether the enthusiasm of this
Victorian era be more conscientious or comical in the multi-
plicity of its shrines and the inconsistency of its articles of
belief, we leave to be decided by the holders of 'the real mes-
meric truth.'" At least the critic recognizes that with its
contradictions this nevertheless *is* an era (and, by the way, his
is a fairly early use, in this self-appraising year which saw the
Great Exhibition, of the adjective *Victorian* to define an age—
much earlier than the first one given, dated 1875, by the *Oxford
English Dictionary*).

body of beliefs is dominant in this era. Optimism versus despair, faith versus criticism, Hebraism versus Hellenism: the list of polarities could go on and on. Whatever Victorianism may be, it is marked not by a set of assumptions but by a complex or a range of moods, even by a process of dialogue, of internal debate. The clues to this range or process, furthermore, lie as much in the way men write or speak as in all that they flatly say.

There are certain subjects, of course, that fairly often recur in Victorian literature: the necessity of work, the importance of both cultural order and individual freedom, the place of woman in society, as well as more abstractly philosophical themes.[3] But for the moment we might consider, instead of subject or theme, two matters of tone and technique that have been suggested as typically Victorian, to see whether they are relevant to a reading of Hopkins. First, there is the feeling of self-consciousness in the literature of nineteenth-century England, a feeling which many Victorians rec-

---

[3] One theme is time, for Carlyle the infinite mystery and the principle of illusion, but for Mill the one reality, and for Newman the real creation of an eternal reality. Almost all major Victorian artists are intensely aware of this "fourth dimension," of personal time and of geological, historical, and, so to speak, evolutionary time as well; of "hard times" and of the progressive movements of these times; of the present perplexing moment and of its possible eternal meaning. On this subject see Jerome H. Buckley's *The Triumph of Time* (Cambridge, Mass., 1966).

ognized and which is embodied in the simultaneous self-probing and self-masking of so much Victorian literature. Second, there is the curiously ambivalent attitude toward the natural, temporal world, an ambivalence embodied in the imagery, both literal and metaphorical, of Victorian writers. In both their self-consciousness and their mixed feelings about things in the landscape, Victorian artists are reacting to, testing, and often radically qualifying the early faiths of so many Romantic poets. For most of those in the post-Romantic generations, the relationship between ego and image, or self and nature, is a tense, problematic one, and not the harmonious interaction, the perfectly mutual give-and-take, that Wordsworth once believed in. One of the best means of showing this relationship, especially in Victorian poetry, is just to consider the tone and detail in passages of natural imagery. It may be especially worthwhile to do this with the poetry of Hopkins; indeed, that is what this study will try to do. But we can begin by touching on the larger subject, less obviously relevant and yet very relevant to Hopkins. We can begin, that is, with the idea introduced by Victorian critics, and supported by some recent critics, about Hopkins' era: the idea that in a particular sense the period from the 1830s through the 1880s is the most self-conscious of all periods in English literary history.

In elaborating on the point, we have to make a contrast between the earlier, Romantic, consciousness of self and this characteristic of the Victorians. When

Carlyle and John Stuart Mill write of self-consciousness as a demon to be avoided, they are apparently combining two meanings in that term: fascination with oneself and uncertainty about oneself. They tend to superimpose the latter, Victorian, sense on the former and thus to obscure what is for English literature if not for others a real distinction. The English Romantics were deeply concerned with their own personalities. The consciousness of self meant for them the most complete awareness of that living universe which the human mind in part apprehends and in part creates. This consciousness could be a source of joy or of suffering, as a man chose one means or another to experience identity with the cosmos. Romantic egoism would absorb all existence into the expanding self. Romantic melancholy, leading to self-annihilation, would allow the individual consciousness to be absorbed into the Infinite. But awareness of self, whether expressed in the sublime egoism of Wordsworth or in the melancholy and self-forgetfulness of Keats, becomes something else in the art of the Victorians.

The difference can be indicated first of all by reference to that extraordinary work which stands at the boundary between Romantic and Victorian, Carlyle's *Sartor Resartus.* Here, in the vatic tones and the organic imagery of the Romantics, Carlyle preaches self-surrender, along with faith in an Infinite to which the self can be surrendered. And yet *Sartor Resartus* is not a prose *Prelude:* introducing irony, ambiguity, and fictional indirection into the narrative, it uses tone and a method of spiritual autobiography that contrast strikingly with Wordsworth's. Perhaps the one part of *The Prelude* that could be said to reveal by disguising a personal experience is the flimsy tale of Vaudracour and Julia, and if its intention is to represent without disclosing the poet's affair with Annette Vallon, that intention was probably disguised to the poet as much as to the reader. But Carlyle is all disguise, all fictional and personal at once, at once indirect and direct, mocking and sincere. Even the Romantic irony of Byron's *Don Juan*, which like *Childe Harold's Pilgrimage* has its share of fictionalized autobiography, is not quite the same, although the Byronic combination of a fine Romantic longing with Augustan stringency predicts Victorian reactions to Wordsworth's faith.[4] The difference is that Byron's

---

[4] Some Victorian critics, at least, saw a tenuous link between Byron's love of dramatizing himself and their own poets' use of dramatic method for essentially personal verse. William Rossetti, in his review of Arnold's *Strayed Reveller* volume, for the second number of *The Germ*, hints at such a link: "If any one quality may be considered common to all living poets, it is that which we have heard aptly described as *self-consciousness*. In this many apppear to see the only permanent trace of the now old usurping deluge of Byronism; but it is truly a fact of the time,—less a characteristic than a portion of it." Apparently Rossetti refers here to the poet's pouring out his heart and soul. Carlyle's injunction "Close thy Byron, open thy Goethe" was not, perhaps, universally heeded, although like his doctrine of anti-self-consciousness it reflects the peculiarly Victorian desire to objectify the ego if not to escape from the bower of Shalott.

irony undercuts emotions, not beliefs. At best he
archieves a nice balance between Romantic sensibility
and critical intelligence, but he does not suggest a division within the intelligence itself, as so many Victorians
do.

With *Sartor Resartus* something new and strange
occurs. Autobiography becomes a means not only of
revealing the mind in its development as in Wordsworth, not only of expressing opinions as in Coleridge's
Biographia Literaria, not only of satirizing mankind as
in Byron, but also—for Carlyle does all this and more
—of asking the question "Who am I?" Carlyle's fictional method of projecting two selves, the puzzled
editor and the puzzling professor, allows for a confronting of the self in the mirror by the questioning
self, of me by I; it implies, as much as the doubly
significant name of Diogenes Teufelsdröckh does, duality, irony, and doubt. In a word, it expresses what we
ordinarily mean in conversation by self-consciousness:
not Romantic egoism or simple fascination with oneself
but a nervous, sometimes stuttering or fluttering awareness of one's hands and feet, uncertainty about how one
looks, about whether one quite belongs here. Something
like this is what Mill and his contemporaries very often
mean by the term. "I am" was the great Romantic
assertion, whether or not it was sublimated in the idea
of an over-soul; "Who am I?" is the great Victorian
question, and it can easily be translated into the simpler
question "Am I?" in a time when the assumptions of

both Descartes and Wordsworth have to be doubted.

Just how nervous Carlyle's questioning is, he indicates by preaching in the voice of Teufelsdröckh against "self-consciousness." The irony that an intensely mannered and self-conscious spiritual autobiography delivers this message is one echoed in a good many other Victorian works; in Tennyson's "Two Voices" and sometimes in his *In Memoriam*, in Ruskin's *Praeterita*, and also in Newman's *Apologia* and Mill's less evidently artful but highly selective and ordered autobiography.[5] In all of these documents, except per-

[5] The framework of *In Memoriam*, with a hymn at the beginning and type of epithalamion at the end, suggests a process of sublimation; but for the most part Tennyson is too direct in the poem to attempt any disguising of emotion and experience, and so it may all be a revelation, but it is not a pose that reveals. Even in "The Two Voices," a revelation of conflict is dramatized only slightly: the "dialogue of the mind with itself" (in Arnold's phrase) is evidently in some sense the poet's own. On dialogue and doubleness in Tennyson, see Allan Danzig, "The Contraries: A Central Concept in Tennyson's Poetry," *PMLA*, LXXVII (1962), 577–585. Ruskin's reordering of his background and early life has been pointed out by Helen Viljoen, who in *Ruskin's Scottish Heritage* (Urbana, Ill., 1956) comments on his *Praeterita* as a work "marked by irony," in which, for instance, the young figure of his mother "is predominantly a character whom he himself created" (p. 25). At least one critic has referred to the volumes of *Modern Painters as* "spiritual autobiography," suggesting even there the intensely personal strain within a grandly generalized form. See Francis G. Townsend, *Ruskin and the Landscape Feeling* (Urbana, Ill., 1951), pp. 5 ff. Walter Houghton's *The Art of Newman's Apologia*, (New Haven, 1945), especially in Chap-

haps Ruskin's, an experience is described, which Jerome
H. Buckley calls "the pattern of conversion," a movement from doubt and isolation toward some faith in the
value of life.[6] In all except Newman's, however, conversion may seem partial and imagined rather than the
total acceptance of an answer to that worrisome question, as posed in Arnold's words, of "what I am and
what I ought to be."

Again and again the combination of autobiography
and art, of direct statement and dramatic indirection, of
uneasy self-awareness and a consequent need to adopt
some impersonal disguise (which fails to be complete
disguise) occurs in Victorian literature. Sometimes, depending on the clarity and artfulness of the dramatic
method, the result is an impressive representation of
human life with its moral ambiguities and mixed feelings. The painfully self-conscious performer, emotion-
ally committed to his role, who turns stage fright into
energy through his art can be more moving than the too
calm master technician. Sometimes, too, the result of
this nervous combination is vagueness, shrillness, or in-

---

ter XI, emphasizes Newman's skill as a "dramatist." As for Mill,
the best-known part of his *Autobiography*, so St. John Packe
argues, is a concentrated and intensified version of one trying
period, dramatically recalled as "A Crisis in My Mental
History." See *The Life of John Stuart Mill* (New York, 1954),
pp. 79–80. The version is effective as literature, certainly; it
has literary parallels; and it may reveal more about Mill than
a less artful transcription of events would.

[6] See Buckley's *The Victorian Temper*, pp. 87–108.

coherence. In *The Buried Life*, taking his title from Arnold's poem about the doubleness of all human beings, Gordon Ray has demonstrated how the novels of Thackeray may draw strength or, at other points, may suffer from precisely this relationship between personal attitude and fictional embodiment.[7]

If, as Professor Ray shows us, Pendennis is Thackeray himself revealed and disguised, entered into and then objectively examined rather as Teufelsdröckh is, surely the boys and young men in Dickens are quite as much the projections of their creator. Before finishing *David Copperfield* the novelist wrote, "I seem to be sending some part of myself into the shadowy world." And, as Edgar Johnson observes, his decision "to make the story of David Copperfield at least in part his own story" enabled Dickens "at the same time to reveal and conceal the dark unhealed wounds that he could not expose without disguise, to analyze, to assess, and to assuage." [8]

Other examples of how the Victorian novelist can use most private experience—Charlotte Brontë's *Villette* for one, and for another Meredith's *Evan Harrington*—suggest that the body of Victorian semifictional

[7] *The Buried Life* (Cambridge, Mass.), 1952.

[8] *Charles Dickens: His Tragedy and Triumph* (New York, 1952), II, 661. See also Chapter VI, pp. 677–700, for Johnson's critical comment on art and autobiography in the novel. The most widely-known essay on the autobiographical element in Dickens is Edmund Wilson's, in his *The Wound and The Bow* (Boston, 1941).

autobiography is complemented by a larger body of Victorian semiautobiographical fiction. It seems clear that no earlier period produced many instances of such fiction; and, although Proust, Gide, and perhaps Joyce as well might be called autobiographical novelists, it seems doubtful that so many important novels of this quite self-conscious kind have been written in English since the Victorians.

But it is the poetry of the age that demonstrates most often its doubleness of mind, its anxious mood of introspection and uncertainty. Like the novelist, of course, the poet may both reveal in part and hide in part quite personal experiences—as Rossetti apparently does in cryptic verses from the *House of Life*.[9] He may, furthermore, express self-consciousness in fantasy or vision.

From Tennyson's "Two Voices" to Clough's version of himself as "Dipsychus," the fantasies and visions of Victorian poetry display a fascination with the dual self.[10] Often, the poet's method reveals the duality im-

[9] In his fairly unsympathetic biography, subtitled *A Victorian Romantic* (New Haven, 1949), Oswald Doughty analyzes parts of *The House of Life* as disguised expressions of the poet's feelings, especially his love for Janie Morris. "His almost paradoxical aim was to reveal yet conceal the most personally significant because most deeply emotional phases of his experience." See also, for a more subtle and sympathetic treatment, the recent biography by R. Glynn Grylls (London, 1966).

[10] Commenting on both Clough's sense of "anti-heroism and the loss of identity" and his ability to "see two sides to every

plicit in Carlyle's being editor and edited, in Thackeray's being narrator and hero. At its grimmest, the sense
of the poet looking anxiously at himself occurs in James
Thomson's "City of Dreadful Night":

> As I came through the desert thus it was,
> As I came through the desert: I was twain,
> Two selves distinct that cannot join again;
> One stood apart and knew but could not stir,
> And watched the other stark in swoon. . . .

At its most whimsical, the poet's self-consciousness is
suggested by these lines:

> "How pleasant to know Mr. Lear!"
>   Who has written such volumes of stuff!
> Some think him ill-tempered and queer,
>   But a few think him pleasant enough.

Edward Lear does not quite commit himself on himself
—as T. S. Eliot comes nearer in our day to doing with

---

question," Walter Houghton suggests, surprisingly, that his
"double vision" was "rare in his own age." What may be rare
(before 1860) is Clough's direct explicit rendering of the
double vision: like Hopkins', though in a very different style,
his verse is highly conscious of self-consciousness. Henry
Sidgwick's 1869 comment on Clough, quoted by Houghton,
seems apposite: "His point of view and habit of mind are less
singular in England in the year 1869 than they were in 1859,
and much less than they were in 1849. We are growing year
by year more introspective and self-conscious: the current
philosophy leads us to a close, patient, and impartial observation and analysis of our mental processes." See *The Poetry
of Clough* (New Haven, 1963), pp. 226–227.

his version, "How unpleasant to meet Mr. Eliot"—but the looking-glass remains at hand.

An even more subtle and pervasive effect of this fascination with and uncertainty about oneself is the Victorian form of dramatic verse which Kristian Smidt has described as "diagonal" or oblique.[11] In this verse it is difficult to be certain how much Tennyson's own feeling enters into the madman's voice of *Maud* or Browning's into the young lover's voice in "Love Among the Ruins," or Arnold's into the voice of his suicide Empedocles. Browning, of course, began his career with a spiritual autobiography, *Pauline*, inspiring Mill to ascribe to him "a more intense and morbid self-consciousness than I ever knew in any sane human being." Whether or not the poet's shift to an apparently objective form, dramatic monologue, is a result of Mill's remark, the effect of his using a dramatic form is sometimes only to disguise personal convictions and even personal experiences—the experience, for instance, of an escape with the beloved from her oppressive home into a fuller life, an escape which is echoed in *The Ring and the Book* when Pompilia flees with Caponsacchi.[12]

[11] *English Studies*, XXXVIII (1957), 1-12.

[12] Acknowledging that it is . . . risky to read autobiography in any imaginative work," Browning's most recent critic, Park Honan, goes on to comment that the poet "appears to have used the characters of Sordello, Paracelsus, and Pauline's speaker to work out problems relating to his own career as an artist." See *Browning's Characters* (New Haven, 1961), p. 80. But the personal note sounds everywhere in Browning, not only in the

Tennyson's methods for disguising his most personal involvement in his art include the use not only of dramatic monologue but also of incantation and trance. He was led through the most intense self-consciousness to a selfless abstraction, by repeating his own name until its individual meaning was unreal.[13] Here again, the poet transforms his own identity, and yet is fascinated by it.

The question of identity is the beginning of self-consciousness. And for the Victorians, as for their readers, it is likely to remain a question. When we ask whether Carlyle is really Professor Teufelsdröckh, whether Dickens is David Copperfield, whether Browning is Sordello, we can of course have no final answer. Or the answer is only that a peculiarly Victorian absorption in and questioning of one's own nature are expressed in poses and in partial disguises—and that they issue, for better or worse, in ambiguity.

There are several ways of misjudging this ambiguity. One, that of the debunker, is to assume that it means mere hypocrisy on the part of Victorian preachers and poets, hypocrisy that vitiates their writing. But by now such a simple-minded attitude has probably gone out of

statements of ideas, as Francis Palgrave observed late in the century: "How seldom does Browning—despite his disclaimers —escape from Browning! Often, one might say, if he has one eye upon his subject, the other is on himself." See *Landscape in Poetry from Homer to Tennyson*, (London, 1897) pp. 264–265.

[13] See Buckley's *Tennyson: The Growth of a Poet* (Cambridge, Mass., 1960), p. 15, which comments on information in Hallam Tennyson's *Memoir*, I, 311.

fashion. Another is to separate neatly the two sides of each writer's personality: to accept as Carlyle's the irony of *Sartor* but not its foggy philosophy; as Thackeray's the charm of his novels but not their sentimentalism; as Browning's the verve of his poems but not their optimism. To do this is, in effect, to oppose artistic integrity, the life of the imagination to the demands of a philistine world; and this is one theme of E. D. H. Johnson's *Alien Vision of Victorian Poetry*, a book with admirable insights and remarkably good passages but one that suffers from overstatement of that theme.[14] For the source of such ambiguities found in Victorian poetry and prose is often, to re-emphasize the point, a self-conscious uncertainty about what the speaker thinks and feels, about what and who, in fact, he is. If there is alienation in Victorian literature it is usually a partial alienation of the artist not only from society but from himself—an alienation caused not so much by the public as by the state of his mind.

There are familiar explanations of why this should be so. Probably, as Walter Houghton suggests, the two great factors are a sense that society is in transition (Victorians originated the idea of an "age of transition," now a cliché applied to almost any age) and a disturbing loss of generally accepted Christian faith. Men rely for their identities on knowing their places in society and in the universe, on the sense of belonging

---

[14] Princeton, 1952.

both in a class and in a greater creation. But thoughtful
Victorians have to ask themselves what their place is
and if they are even creatures. Arthur Carr has recently
pointed out that until sometime in the nineteenth century the assumed doctrine of the Incarnation gave significance to individual lives, but that now this doctrine
could no longer be taken for granted, even by New
man.[15] One other point: men are also given lasting identities by relationships within the family. If I am not the
son of God, if I am not a farmer by virtue of being a
farmer's child, still I remain my father's son. Certainly
the last of stable institutions to be questioned by Victorians were marriage and the family. Still, we may possibly doubt G. M. Young's assertion that Victorian belief
in the family was not generally shaken; or at least we
may remember that the grounds and nature of marriage, and especially the role of the wife, are serious
problems for many later Victorians, and not only for
Mill or Meredith.[16] Furthermore, the alienation of sons
from their fathers in Arnold's "Sohrab and Rustum," in
Meredith's *Richard Feverel*, and in Butler's technically
post-Victorian *Way of All Flesh* would suggest another aspect of the problem. Men who practice the
self-examination which Headmaster Arnold and

[15] See Arthur Carr's introduction to *Victorian Poetry:
Clough to Kipling* (New York, 1959), pp. x–xi.
[16] See G. M. Young's *Victorian England* (London, 1936),
p. 150.

George Eliot's Evangelicals preach may remain uncertain about what value or order or person defines the self as it is and ought to be.[17]

Self-conscious Victorians may sometimes be naive.

[17] But many of the doubts which characterize the nineteenth century have a place in our world as well. What, then, is the difference between Victorian self-consciousness and modern anxiety about the personal "image?" It is often, I think, the difference between earnest questioning and quite skeptical irony. The ironic tone in Victorian literature usually expresses discomfort instead of either amusement by or resignation to the morally ambiguous nature of things. To put it another way, Victorians are likely to assume that there are truths, hard though they may be, to which one can be converted—including a truth about oneself, a "buried life." And so Victorian art is frequently, and evidently, the artist's attempt to discover himself. In much modern poetry and fiction the attempt is to create oneself, whether through the *personae* of Pound or the various refractions of the southern American in Faulkner. To be sure, those journeys into a personal past which Proust, Mann, Joyce all undertake may tend at least to qualify this general comment; but increasingly in our time, writers speak of invention, of creation, of myth-making to give chaos a significance. Yeats sails to Byzantium in order to make a durable self and not in order to find himself. In some of its most interesting forms, of course, the assumption that a man creates his nature is given voice by all existentialists. Some of its least attractive manifestations are the advertisers' and politicians' appeals to us that invent "images" of ourselves and thus manipulate our desires. In any case, combinations of fictional literature and serious self-projection are less frequent or less obvious today. Sophisticated writers may or may not be reticent in print, but they are likely to be reticent at least in poetry and fiction. Perhaps they have become too conscious of how much art can reveal.

But in asking "who I am and what I ought to be," they are asking after truth. Personal experience and fictional form are repeatedly joined in the posing of this question. For the disguises and the poses in Victorian art are usually not attempts to create anew nor to hide the artist's self, but rather to ask about and perhaps to discover a personal conviction, a personal identity.

And this is what Hopkins' poetry of inscape is about. It is, at its best, more successful than other Victorian poetry in coming to terms with self-consciousness, in controlling doubleness, ambiguity, an ambivalent tone: in fact, at least sometimes, it passes beyond disguises to deal directly with the question of what self is, of what I am. In being so fully conscious of self-consciousness, however, Hopkins does not cease to be self-conscious. Describing his spirit as a bird and his mind as a landscape is a way of projecting personal struggle into public language, one by which the poet can communicate self-doubt that is otherwise too painful to express. It may be a way as well of escaping the fear of solipsism which plagued some other Victorians and could be inspired by Hopkins' own insistence upon inscape, on the unique individuality of self. Furthermore, he combines the most intensely personal quality—special diction, odd syntax, and spiritual autobiography—with his apparently objective matter. The union of personal emotion with Catholic faith is, to be sure, a keynote of the religious lyric. It occurs strikingly in the lyrics of Hopkins' favorite, George Herbert. "The Wreck of the Deutschland," like other long lyrics on religious matters, the fourteenth-century "Pearl" and Milton's ode "On the Morning of Christ's Nativity," deliberately brings individual experience and emotion to the great subject of God's dealings with humankind. Yet "the Deutschland" is marked as a Victorian version of religious poetry by its nervously shifting, fanciful self-revelation—"My heart" is "carrier-witted, I am bold to boast," and then at once, "I am soft sift / In an hour-glass"—and by its need to move from the self to the whole society, the whole nation, addressing God first as "Thou mastering me" and finally as "hero of us," "rare-dear Britain." The poet reveals his sense of self and then enters imaginatively into the suffering of an heroic soul in order to declare a hope for more than self, for "English souls"; but all of this is a means to define, explore, and to generalize upon the nature of self.

If Hopkins, like Newman, differs from most Victorians because his specifically religious conversion was definite, not a fiction, and was a condition preceding rather than a pattern within his major works, he nevertheless resembles other Victorian writers in being unable to forget the self, himself. Repeatedly he asks and answers the question "Who am I?" This is not at all to suggest that he wavers in his faith, in his essentially Christian answer to the question. It is only to say that in his age—when he could no more than Newman suppose the doctrine of the Incarnation to be universally accepted—the question posed itself constantly and in various ways, and so it had to be answered constantly and in various terms. Behind the terms is one answer, paradoxical perhaps and complex in its implications, yet one answer. The answer, however, has to be given in the Victorian language of a writer who cannot help showing some measure of nervous self-examination. His nervousness is not quite typically Jesuit, for Ignatius Loyola's *Spiritual Exercises* aim at overcoming false scruples and morbid self-doubts. It can be, but need not be, characteristic of any religious person. It certainly is characteristic of the mid-Victorian intellectual and artist.

Although autobiography of the circumstantial kind is not frequent in Hopkins, some of his early poems hint at it. The beginning of a pattern of conversion, moving from doubts through a center of uncertainty, if not indifference, to an Everlasting Yea, can be seen in "The Halfway House," written in 1865, in which the "national old Egyptian reed," presumably the Church of England, gives way; and in "Nondum," written in 1866, not long before the poet was received into the Roman Catholic Church by Newman. These and possibly a few passages in other early poems give a hardly disguised expression to the gradual and finally complete conversion.[18]

[18] The "Soliloquy of One of the Spies Left in the Wilderness" was written near the end of Hopkins' first year at Oxford, when he was just passing beyond the stage of being influenced

There are, however, more significant and more painful self-probings later. Hopkins comes to know what Carlyle could never confess: that complete conversion does not completely change the earthly self. Some misunderstandings about Hopkins's life, about the relation between his priestly and poetic vocations, and some serious misreadings of his late anguished verse, the "terrible sonnets," appear to result from certain critics' failure to grasp this fact. But the poet can never cease to be himself or to be self-conscious. Although firmly con-

---

by Balliol liberalism. Although the monologue might signify nothing more than a Victorian interest in the contrast between the wilderness of this present and the paradise of past or future, it ends, with a striking note, "I sicken, I know not why, / And faint as though to die." There certainly seems to be some kind of spiritual autobiography in "The Beginning of the End," an 1865 version of a love poem—rare in the Hopkins canon!—that is in fact a rather Arnoldian non-love poem: he feels, and the statement sounds more than conventional, that love like a favorite poet, "grows less and less sweet to him, and he knows no cause." Finally, and the instance is more important, the 1865 lines beginning "Myself unholy" are unmistakable self-revelation, and they express the Victorian need of Carlyle, Mill, Tennyson, Arnold, and others to escape from melancholy and from isolation, to find an external object of faith which gives meaning to self. The young poet who expects to find holy examples in his friends, friends who are to be like pure doves as he is like a rook, or like fresh brooks as he is like a salt-and-sand-filled stream (are, in fact, to be for him what Hallam is for Tennyson), discovers that they, too, being fallen creatures, have their faults. Human society is not enough:

"No *better* serves me now, save *best: no other*
Save Christ: to Christ I look, on Christ I call."

vinced of the answer to them, he is still affected by anxieties about personal isolation and about the need to justify oneself by work. Lonely, in Ireland, he writes,

> To seem the stranger lies my lot, my life
> Among strangers. Father and mother dear,
> Brother and sisters are in Christ not near
> And he my peace my parting, sword and strife.

Literally separated from home, from the England and family he loves, he feels only more intensely cut off from communion. The nervousness and need are always there, along with the fear that his duty, "dark heaven's baffling ban," may always require being terribly alone. Even more intense is the feeling of temporary isolation from God Himself, what J. Hillis Miller calls the peculiarly nineteenth-century sense of "the Disappearance of God." The modern reader may think of Kafka when he hears the poignant lines, in "I wake and feel the fell of dark, not day,"

> And my lament
> In cries countless, cries like dead letters sent
> To dearest him that lives alas! away.

But the accent is very much that of the Victorian poet. The deep frustration of never quite seeing "behind the veil" is even deeper for a religious man like Hopkins than it is for Tennyson. Finally, the poem expresses an extreme and painful sense of self: God has decreed "my taste [be] rue." This taste of self is bitter, "gall," "heartburn."

> I see
> The lost are like this, and their scourge to be
> As I am mine, their sweating selves; but worse.

As a matter of fact, the last phrase seems to contradict the beginning of another sonnet "written in blood" (possibly but not certainly an earlier poem), "No worst, there is none," by recalling that there always is something worse, damnation and complete alienation from God, than being one's morbid self.

The difficult "Spelt from Sibyl's Leaves" is about the admixture of darkness, death, and evil in the brightness of the physical world, and "Carrion Comfort" is about the poet's refusal to despair, even as he feels impotent and cut off from heaven; these are attempts to qualify and see beyond the "pitch of grief" of the three dark poems, "No worst, there is none," "To seem the stranger lies my lot," and "I wake and feel the fell of dark, not day." But the most pragmatic confrontation of the poet's personal sense of dryness and darkness comes, perhaps, in the lines, beginning "My own heart let me more have pity on." Hopkins fairly often speaks to himself in verse; here, the advice he gives himself, to forget his own bitter "taste," his inadequacy, makes us think of Carlyle and all the other "anti-self-conscious" self-conscious Victorians:

> Soul, self; come, poor Jackself, I do advise
> You, jaded, let be; call off thoughts awhile
> Elsewhere.

He cannot heed the advice.

At the end of a more splendid poem, "That Nature Is a Heraclitean Fire," this "Jackself," "Jack, joke, poor potsherd," is abruptly to become "immortal diamond." The striking fact about Hopkins is that his art is excited to its highest pitch of celebration as it is to its deepest expression of personal suffering by the awareness of the self. His dark poems show an extreme ennui, even horror, of self that is the opposite and complement to his fascination, his delight, with inscape, sheer selfhood. Never pretending that the Everlasting Yea, or Culture, or Work, or Art, or Religion, or anything else can achieve self-forgetfulness, he seems to break into separate radical responses the very two aspects, intense fascination with self and agonizing doubt or despair about self, that together make up what has been meant by Victorian self-consciousness.

> God's most deep decree
> Bitter would have me taste; my taste was me;
> Bones built in me, flesh filled, blood brimmed the curse.
> Selfyeast of spirit a dull dough sours.

And yet,

> Each mortal thing does one thing and the same:
> Deals out that being indoors each one dwells:
> Selves—goes itself; *myself* it speaks and spells;
> Crying *What I do is me: for that I came.*

If these passages, from "I wake and feel the fell of dark" and "As kingfishers catch fire," seem almost to

contradict each other, their reconciliation may be
hinted at by what follows in the "kingfishers" lines:

> I say more: the just man justices;
> Keeps grace: that keeps all his goings graces;
> Acts in God's eye what in God's eye he is—
> Christ.

The individual can be either sour because he is cut off
from his divine source or, through grace, richly inscaped and Christlike. The difference between the two
approximates, as nearly as any contrast on earth can, the
difference between hell and heaven. Selfhood is either
the most hateful thing on earth, as Arnold sometimes
thinks, and Swinburne often feels, or the most splendid
thing on earth, as Browning might say. But for Hopkins
it can be more hateful than for the others, as it can be
more splendid.[19]

---

[19] The poet's intense awareness of self is most directly expressed, perhaps, in his exercises entitled "First Principle and
Foundation" (*Principium sive Fundamentum*), included by
Christopher Devlin, S.J., in *The Sermons and Devotional
Writings of Gerard Manley Hopkins* (London, 1959), pp. 122–
130. Here Hopkins describes his sense of "my selfbeing, my
consciousness and feeling of myself, of *I* and *me* above and
in all things." He considers the individual mind as "selving or
pitch of a great universal mind" and at the same time suggests
the solipsistic problem of "selftaste" that is unique and incom-
municable. But the real individual self is pitched and potential
as well as actual, whereas the real universal or divine, "a self
independent of its selving in other things," is "not selved in or
identified with other things" but is totally "selfexistent." At
the end of his often brilliantly perceptive essay on Hopkins,

The sestet of "No worst, there is none" leads us to the second characteristic attributed to Victorian literature, one especially important for poetry, its use of ambivalent imagery: the mind, now, becomes a landscape that reveals both grandeur and darkness in physical nature.

> O the mind, mind has mountains; cliffs of fall
> Frightful, sheer, no-man-fathomed. Hold them cheap
> May who ne'er hung there. Nor does long our small
> Durance deal with that steep or deep. Here! creep,
> Wretch, under a comfort serves in a whirlwind: all
> Life death does end and each day dies with sleep.

As well as suggesting a certain strain of the morbid in Arnold, Tennyson, and Swinburne, these lines are Vic-

---

J. Hillis Miller seems to be unimpressed by the poet's way of resolving the Victorian fear of being isolated and naturally valueless. He writes that Hopkins is left "with nothing but the 'comfort of the Resurrection,' the hope of that miracle of transubstantiation [that changes the self from one form to another, to the form] actualized by God in ways that are as far apart as the whole distance from hell to heaven." But for Hopkins, living man experiences fallen nature, not hell; all God's modes of action, lovely or awful, can and should lead the faithful man to heaven; and this "nothing but" is everything. See "The Creation of the Self in Gerard Manley Hopkins," *ELH*, XXII (1955), 293–319, especially the last page; and *The Disappearance of God* (Cambridge, Mass., 1963), pp. 270–359. I regard Miller's final views on Hopkins, in both the essay and the chapter, as wrong, but his work, Elisabeth Schneider's several articles, and Geoffrey Hartman's discussions—in *The Unmediated Vision* (New Haven, 1954)—are the most intelligent considerations Hopkins's poetry has received lately.

torian both in giving landscape a distinctly human meaning and in altering its positive Wordsworthian associations. The mountain in Wordsworth—for instance, in the celebrated passage on Mount Snowdon at the beginning of Book Fourteen in *The Prelude*—is often identified with the highest powers of the human mind. Shelley and Keats associate mountains with mysterious grandeur, with the highest imaging-forth of the one power, the one life, in man and nature. But for many Victorians, not only for Ruskin, there is both a "mountain glory" and a "mountain gloom." Hopkins' mountains of the mind have "frightful" cliffs; Arnold's mountains of truth, in "Shakespeare" and in "Rugby Chapel," may be distant and cloudy, and they are also "no-man-fathomed." The whole Romantic landscape has, it seems, been subtly changed in Victorian poetry, not just in the grotesque wastelands of Tennyson's "Vision of Sin," Browning's "Childe Roland," and Thomson's "City of Dreadful Night," but also in the mixed, uneasy metaphors of these and other poets: the Victorian poetic landscape includes mountains that are magnificent but strange or frightening; marvelously attractive whirlwinds and tempests that threaten to destroy men; animals that signify both freedom and mortality; flowers and fruits that are beautiful but morbid and sometimes deadly dangerous; light that is brilliant and often harsh.

At the same time, post-Romantic poets are deeply interested in the out-of-doors world and want faithfully to reproduce it. The Tennyson of *In Memoriam* who knows that nature is "red in tooth and claw" is almost as concerned with being accurate in his description of physical life as he is in responding to its moral meaning or lack of moral meaning.[20] Other poets, if less literal-minded, are no less fascinated by the natural creature, animate or inanimate. Arnold's "Forsaken Merman" and Browning's Caliban provide ambiguous examples of the figure who seems human but perhaps is not: animal nature, raw physical nature, is very close to man's—closer perhaps than he usually cares to suppose. The serpent-woman Geraldine in Coleridge's unfinished "Christabel," like the sea serpents in "The Ancient Mariner" and the serpent-woman Lamia in Keats's poem, may have suggested nature's ultimate alliance with man. But Tennyson's, Arnold's, and Browning's poems can be taken to hint uneasily of Victorian fears that man may be ultimately reducible to mere nature, and they may hint of their reactions to those fears. Beasts, half-beasts, man-like beasts, along with the palpable and closely observed setting of land and sea, intrigue Victorian writers, but the fascinating beasts and attractive settings remain divorced, unblessed, and alien.

As for fruits and flowers, these traditional images also have a double meaning, one more intense than in traditional verse about the bittersweet fruits of this world

[20] See, on this concern for accuracy, Buckley's *The Victorian Temper*, Chapter VII, and especially pp. 134–139.

and lovely but ephemeral roses. In the flower imagery of Tennyson there is repeatedly a sinister feeling, one suggested by the refrain of an early "Song":

> Heavily hangs the broad sunflower
> Over its grave i' the earth so chilly;
> Heavily hangs the hollyhock,
> Heavily hangs the tiger-lily.

The feeling is suggested also by the use of lilies and roses in both *Maud* and the *Idylls of the King,* lilies that are associated with isolation, with passivity, with pale death, and roses that are associated with lust, with violence, with bloody death.[21] The song "A worm within the rose" in "Pelleas and Ettarre," one of the later and more bitterly negative idylls, expresses clearly the poet's sense of corruption in the beautiful images of physical nature. Among the Pre-Raphaelites, both Dante and Christina Rossetti are fascinated by the richest and smallest details in foliage and fruit and are again uneasy about them. "Goblin Market," Christina Rossetti's best-known long poem, tries to abjure the forbidden fruits of earthly indulgence, in spite of the poet's imagery in her more personal lyrics; but once more there is no single simple attitude that is possible, for these forbidden fruits which goblins peddle are almost irresistibly attractive, and the goblins themselves are at least as grotesquely delightful as they are evil, in

[21] On this symbolism, see E. D. H. Johnson's "The Lily and the Rose: Symbolic Meaning in Tennyson's *Maud,*" *PMLA,* LXIV (1949), 1222–1227.

their exuberance: "cat-like and rat-like, Ratel- and wombat-like," "full of airs and graces," they cry out,

> "Look at our apples
> Russet and dun,
> Bob at our cherries,
> Bite at our peaches,
> Citrons and dates,
> Grapes for the asking,
> Pears red with basking
> Out in the sun,
> Plums on their twigs;
> Pluck them and suck them,
> Pomegranates, figs."

Again, the animal-like man who is not quite man seems deeply attractive and has to be denied. Again, the flowers and fruits of earth are tempting and yet somehow, smacking of mortality, are dangerous, are forbidden.

The very sunlight that warms the creature and works for fruitfulness evokes a double response in much of Victorian poetry. All of Tennyson's retiring isolated figures, like the Lady of Shalott, Mariana, and Tithonus, are cut off from the harsh sunshine as they are from human society: at best their lights are cold and at worst dawn seems bleak to them. So it does to the poet himself, alone and grieving, in some of the darkest and most beautiful lines of *In Memoriam:*

> The noise of life begins again,
> And ghastly thro' the drizzling rain
> On the bald street breaks the blank day.

Arnold, in "The New Sirens" and in "Mycerinus," also dramatizes a desire to escape from the blank sunlight of the world outside, into dark lonely places. And it is a desire, often morbid, that Swinburne shares. The very metaphor and image of life and truth, for Milton, the Augustans, and Wordsworth, can be for the Victorians uncertain, and can invite ambivalent responses.

It may be that the combination of deep interest in the images of nature and anxiety about them, or need to exert control over them and thus, as it were, to keep the landscape safe, is reflected in English painting of this age as well as in poetry and prophecy.[22] Mid-Victorian art, between the later years of Turner in the 1840s and the flourishing of Whistler in the 1870s and 1880s, shows very little wild Romantic nature, very few scenes of tempestuous oceans or vast and distant mountains.[23] When mid-Victorian pictures include landscape, it is likely to be reduced to a small part of the canvas, or

[22] The tendency of this painting, from the 1840s (the last decade of Turner's career) until the 1870s was to emphasize human foregrounds, to produce narrative or illustrative scenes with human interest, and either to make landscape sketchy and subordinate or to use it for its symbolic and psychological relevance to the people in the picture. John Steegman observes that from the 1830s "through most of the century" the three main kinds of English painting were genre, illustrative, and historical. Both portraiture and landscape had lesser importance than genre. See *Consort of Taste 1830–1870* (London, 1950), p. 14.

[23] But there was a revival of interest in landscape and especially in seascape during the last three decades of the century.

is selected for its relevance to a human foreground. Even Holman Hunt's celebrated "Scape Goat," painted in the most faithful detail on the salt flats of the Dead Sea, is essentially concerned, for all the literalness of its creator's intention, with the moral, literary, and entirely human meaning of the animal and scene. An equally famous, even better picture from these decades when landscape has less importance than genre, illustrative, and historical painting, is Madox Brown's "The Blind Girl"; and in that work by the Victorian artist who is best at oil landscapes, the whole brilliant out-of-doors setting, the sky and field and butterfly on the blind girl's shawl, exist in order to give pathos to, and to focus upon, the human figure.

In spite of his love for landscape, his early Wordsworthian "landscape feeling," John Ruskin has something to do with this general reduction of sea and land to a subsidiary place in art, for his most influential criticism insists upon the moral significance of all the arts in a way that encourages anecdotal and illustrative pictures.[24] In his famous chapter in *Modern Painters* on

[24] Ruskin, the defender of Turner, surprised some of his contemporaries by praising such canvases as Holman Hunt's "The Awakening Conscience," the vivid and conventionally moral *genre* picture of a fallen woman and her lover. Painting, Ruskin declares, is beginning "to take its proper place beside literature," and this picture is one of the "first fruits of its new effort." See *Modern Painters*, III, Part VII, sec. 18; and, for an account of this strain in Victorian art criticism and the reaction to it, my paper "The Bride of Literature: Ruskin, the East-

"The Pathetic Fallacy," Ruskin insists that the highest
order of literary artist recognizes the literal and separate
existence of things in nature, knowing that water, sky,
and trees do not feel as men do. Displaying high
Victorian concern for truth, and disregarding the early
Wordsworth's half-serious belief that flowers indeed
have feelings, Ruskin agrees with the Coleridge of "Dejection" that nature shares our emotions only in our
fancy, has only the human significance we project into
it; and he does not always or entirely approve of this
projection. It is a hard conclusion for the Victorians to
reach, one that Arnold often wrestles with, for it gives
to landscape an alien and frightening quality. And it
does so in an age of geological and biological investiga-
tions that already tend to make the world of nature
strange, inhuman. Joy in the landscape is difficult now;
cataclysmic upheavals, the bestial nature of creature
existence, the meaningless mortality of species, as of
earth's flowers and fruits, the often cruel, cold and
foreign light of day, are hard to forget and may have to
be kept under control. Nature, as John Stuart Mill
observes, is as bad as it is good from man's point of
view, and it needs to be directed.[25]

lakes, and Mid-Victorian Theories of Art, in the *Victorian
Newsletter*, Fall, 1964, 23–28.

[25] See his essay entitled "Nature," one of the *Three Essays
on Religion* published posthumously in 1874. This essay, however, was probably written before 1855, and certainly before
1859, when Darwin's *On the Origin of Species* was published.
The final paragraph begins, "The scheme of Nature regarded

Not that Ruskin himself quite agrees. And Ruskin's influence, in some aspects at least of his perhaps self-contradictory preachments, is an important one on Hopkins. As a young man the poet wanted to be a Pre-Raphaelite painter; that is, following the advice of the great art critic, he wanted to be minutely faithful to each particular form of visible nature, whether the nature of landscape or that of man. Indeed, Hopkins' idea of *inscape,* a term apparently modeled on the word *landscape,* resulted in part from this influence. "Landscape feeling" in Hopkins may almost seem a religion. It certainly seems a religion in the early and influential parts of *Modern Painters*—influential, in this respect, on the theory if not on the practice of Pre-Raphaelite and other Victorian painters.[26]

His drawings reveal Hopkins's almost Pre-Raphaelite love of detail: some could be by Holman Hunt and one or two even suggest Ford Madox Brown.[27] His juvenile

---

in its whole extent, cannot have had, for its sole or even principle object, the good of human or other sentient beings. What good it brings to them, is mostly the result of their own exertions."

[26] See Francis G. Townsend, *Ruskin and the Landscape Feeling* (Urbana, Ill., 1951).

[27] Some of these drawings are reproduced in *The Journals and Papers of Gerard Manley Hopkins,* ed. Humphry House and Graham Storey (London, 1959). See, for Hopkins' assertion of his own artistic ambitions, *Further Letters of Gerard Manley Hopkins,* ed. Claude C. Abbott (2d ed., London, 1956), p. 214 (a letter of 20 July 1864). See also, for a discussion of the Pre-Raphaelites' and, especially, Ruskin's influence, Alan

verse betrays the same early interests. A boyhood poem "The Escorial," for instance, reads like the description of a mid-Victorian exotic canvas though it smuggles in as well a sixth stanza upon Gothic architecture. And "Winter with the Gulf Stream" is a clearly detailed seasonal portrait. Certain early verses, it is true, have absorbed another style of richness: "The Habit of Perfection" sounds like Keats converted to asceticism, with its lines, "Elected Silence, sing to me," "Pipe me to pastures still and be / The music that I care to hear," and "Palate, the hutch of tasty lust, / Desire not to be rinsed with wine." But his sharp-eyed delight in all the odd and small phenomena of nature, including each vein in the ivy on the wall and the precise "gear and tackle" of every trade, may well be Hopkins' inheritance from Ruskin and from the very earliest theories of the Pre-Raphaelite brotherhood. One of Hopkins' great themes is also theirs, the beauty of things as they are. And, one could add, of actual places: the poet's devotion to place is evident in his passages and poems on Wales, such as "Penmaen Pool," and in his lines "To Oxford" and "Duns Scotus's Oxford." He praises God, as Ruskin might, for "dappled things," for everything original and strange, for opposites like "swift, slow; sweet, sour; adazzle, dim"—in one phrase, for "landscape plotted and pieced."

Yet, like the other poets of his age, Hopkins sees that

Heuser's *The Shaping Vision of Gerard Manley Hopkins* (London, 1958), especially pp. 9–22.

landscape may be darkened, may be ravaged, and, after all, has "no heart to feel." Like the painters of his age, Hopkins can at last reduce landscape to a background for the human self. This appears to be so even in "Ribblesdale," a poetic echo to several passages in Ruskin on how men pollute clear water and corrupt sweet land.[28]

> Earth, sweet Earth, sweet landscape with leaves throng
> And louchèd low grass
>
> . . . . .
>
>   strong
> Thy plea with him who dealt, nay does now deal
> Thy lovely dale down thus and thus bids reel
> Thy river, and o'er gives all to rack and wrong.
>
> . . . . .
>
> And what is Earth's eye, tongue, or heart else, where
> Else but in dear and dogged man?

The point of asking this question is the point arrived at, too, by the later Ruskin, who comes to care even more for dogged man than for landscape in art and nature. To be sure, "Ribblesdale" goes on to blame man, "to his own selfbent so bound," for being "thriftless" and laying waste to landscape. The emphasis is still largely on the possible meaning of nature, its intrinsic beauty and its expression of divine beauty—as well as, at the end,

[28] For instance, Letter V (1 May 1871) of *Fors Clavigera*, on the three material things essential to life, pure air, water, and earth. Ruskin declares that all three are vitiated, or fouled, in nineteenth-century England. Another striking passage, on clean water and its pollution by men, is at the beginning of Ruskin's Introduction to *The Crown of Wild Olive* (1866).

its seeming concern for men that amounts to pathetic fallacy. But the primacy of mankind is established, to be developed beyond this point in the later "That Nature Is a Heraclitean Fire."

Furthermore, for all his delight in the minutiae of physical nature, Hopkins has to realize, as so many other Victorians have to, that this nature is sometimes stormy, that animal beauty is distracting and ephemeral, that every flower and fruit is merely mortal, and that the source of light is the source also of blinding, blasting energy. The realization is just as hard for him as for any other nineteenth-century poet; in fact, it may be harder than for almost any other. Although his half-Romantic love of nature is grounded in Christian belief, and this is the difference that allows him to be reconciled to the facts of mortality and evil, Hopkins is more reluctant than almost any of his contemporaries to see the world of landscape and animal as a fallen world. This priest and poet is less inclined to be a moralist, in the usual narrow sense of the term, than his secular fellows. He sees God's grandeur in the flesh and the world, and, answering his own question, "To What Serves Mortal Beauty?" he passes over the traditional preacher's subject of carnal temptation with hardly more than the one adjective "dangerous." But he is forced to stop short, again and again, and to realize mournfully how inadequate, how brief, for all their appeal, the beauties of the flesh and the world are.

In these and in other respects, Hopkins is like his

contemporaries. As the Victorians are a group of men and women who disagree with each other—if not each within his own work—in style, in temperament, and in belief, Hopkins is like his contemporaries in being unlike them; yet he does share with almost all Victorian writers certain difficulties of personal tone and certain problems of confronting nature. In other ways, too, he belongs to his age. Like other Victorian poets, he displays an early Romantic strain, showing the influence of Wordsworth and of Keats—both poets are referred to in his 1864–1865 fragments of "Richard"—and attempting a Romantic ballad in 1864, with "The Queen's Crowning." [29] He makes use of the Victorian dramatic forms of soliloquy and monologue: a fragmentary "Pilate" and an interesting "Soliloquy of One of the Spies Left in the Wilderness" in 1864, and, in 1865, "The Alchemist in the City," and an answer to Christina Rossetti's *Convent Threshold*, "A Voice from the World," as well as a quite late projected play, "St. Winefred's Well." He even tries one or two portraits of characters, "Felix Randal" in 1880, and in 1887 "Tom's Garland," a rare, somewhat oblique, comment on social order and social injustice. Finally, he touches

[29] W. H. Gardner points out, in his fourth edition p. 305, the resemblance of these verses to several ballads in the Child collection. This edition, *Poems of Gerard Manley Hopkins* ed. W. H. Gardner and Norman H. MacKenzie (enlarged, with additional notes, London, 1967), is the source for all quotations from the poetry.

on the theme of marriage, a major theme for both
Tennyson and Browning, in two late poems, "At the
Wedding March," and the beautiful uncompleted "Epithalamion." In all of these verses, some early and some
late, the poet is himself aware of his relationship with
contemporary poets. Even when he is intimating Milton, in "Il Mystico," he is afraid of plagiarizing Tennyson.[30] (As Arnold once remarked, the influence was
hard to escape: most mid- and late-Victorian poets simply had Tennyson singing in their heads.) Yet, after all,
the less obvious and more significant fact for his major
poetry is the fact that Hopkins and the other Victorians
share with each other no specific beliefs or negations of
belief, no particular literary forms or sets of assumptions as to God, man, and nature, but rather an oblique,
often nervous, constantly self-questioning manner and a
deep feeling of ambivalence about the sea, the sky, the
seasonal trees, flowers, and fruits, the very light of
day—about the whole Romantic landscape.

[30] Gardner quotes from a letter by Hopkins to E. H. Coleridge: " 'In *Il Mystico* I had formerly . . . "And when the
silent heights were won, Alone in air to face the sun." Now
is that or is it not plagiarism from Tennyson's *Eagle* "Close
to the sun in lonely lands," (see the poem)? I am in that state
that I want an unprejudiced decision.' " The lines in the final
version are, "And when the silent height were won, / And
all in lone air stood the sun." See, in the fourth edition (among
the "Unfinished Poems, Fragments"), the poem, p. 113 and
the note, p. 297.

2 "The Wreck of the Deutschland"

Hopkins' longest poem, his first major poem, includes both an introspective, self-conscious strain and a Victorian version of a Romantic setting. Although "The Wreck of the Deutschland" was inspired by the newspaper account of a shipwreck in which five German nuns died, the work is largely a personal revelation. In some respects startlingly unconventional, it is yet another instance of the Victorian poet's combining introspective manner with dramatic matter; but the result is not so much oblique or ambiguous as it is complex. The personal, spiritual, experience and the imagined experience of the five women on a sinking ship are equal subjects, and he shifts from one to the other, trying at first and at last to relate himself to his narrative.

"The Deutschland," then, is an extended personal lyric, although it is much more than that as well. It is certainly not a dramatic monologue. The first person singular pronoun in its various forms, *I*, *me*, and *my*, occurs, outside quotation marks, nearly thirty times in these thirty-five stanzas—mostly but not entirely in the first part. There can be no doubt that each time it refers to the poet himself. In the eighteenth stanza he addresses his own heart as *you*. And the fairly frequent uses of *we* and *us*, although they mean men in general, "all of us," or Englishmen in general, "English souls," also involve the poet personally in his reflections and prayers.

Still, the poem tends to move from the personal to the dramatic—with now and then a shift back to the poetic speaker—and from one man's religious experience to the spiritual state of the nation. It may not quite recapitulate in this form, say, Browning's movement from the apparent self-analysis of his earliest poems to the apparent dramatic objectivity of his monologues; but this tendency does at least suggest Hopkins' need to project the self by seeming to enter into the experiences of other persons.

If the double emphasis upon the personal and the dramatic in "The Deutschland" makes Hopkins seem a poet of his times, then so does the quality of its setting and its imagery. His beginning with and then moving way from pure introspection, that intense Romantic awareness of self which for so many Victorians becomes uncomfortable, are closely related to the poet's way of seeing physical nature, and specifically the ocean. The ocean is not now a Romantic image for the profound idea of Nature or for the Over-soul; it is a place where men can suffer and die. The Victorian poet tries to look away from himself, to look out at the world of men and natural objects; and his imagination cannot identify itself with everything there, for he remains partly alien from and partly fearful of the sky, the land, and the sea.

In fact, Romantic seascape, even more than Romantic landscape, poses difficulties for Victorian artists. When Ruskin writes of the second order of poets who delight in a "pathetic fallacy," he cites Coleridge, Wordsworth, and Keats with more approval than "cold-hearted Pope," but he makes it quite clear that Keats's "modern" way of ascribing indolence to the waves is inferior to the Homeric, literally truthful way of seeing the ocean—and nearly half of Ruskin's examples of pathetic fallacy are from seascape passages. He is applying to seascape as well as to landscape the disillusioned attitude of Coleridge's "Dejection": the moral imperative of truth-telling makes us declare that the waters have no human feelings, or, as Arnold is to conclude so plaintively in "Dover Beach," sea nature has "really neither joy, nor love, nor light, / Nor certitude, nor peace, nor help for pain." In such a passage there is much more than Mill's calm recognition that physical nature is indifferent to man and must be directed by him. There is a poignant, painful turning away from the grandest Romantic image of natural coherence, a sharp questioning of what W. H. Auden calls the distinctive Romantic attitude with its desire to "leave the land and the city"; there is an unnerving sense that if "the sea is the real situation and the voyage is the true condition of man," his situation is isolated and his condition is terribly frightening.[1] This turning away, this questioning of the great Romantic ocean, an image that both attracts and frightens the poet, occur repeatedly in Arnold and Clough; and a similar double response to the sea as "Mighty Mother" and yet an unfeeling and destructive force is apparent as well in the imagery of Tennyson and especially that of Swinburne.

The setting for "The Wreck of the Deutschland" is a stormy ocean, and the waters of that ocean are as dark and alien to man's earthly self, as any in Arnold, Tennyson, or Swinburne. Furthermore, the poet's attitude toward his seascape might, like theirs, be called profoundly ambivalent. His poem is dedicated to "the happy memory" of five nuns "drowned between midnight and morning of Dec. 7th, 1875"; and their memory is happy because they have been tested and proved by the God Who is "sway of the sea." The syntax means not only that He holds sway but also that He *is* this elemental force in one of its several aspects. And the sea does have several aspects. The difference be-

[1] See Auden's *The Enchafèd Flood* (London, 1951), p. 23, for a definition of the "Romantic attitude" that relates these ideas to the iconography of the ocean and of the desert.

tween Hopkins' ocean and that of Wordsworth, Coleridge, or Shelley is that the familiar imagery has now
come to represent not imagined Oneness, but experienced doubleness. Coleridge's ancient mariner underwent a moral revelation on the sea by recognizing how
the apparently alien creatures of the deep could be
blessed, how their lives were one with his human life.
The nun who is Hopkins' heroine undergoes a suffering
and trial on the sea that require us to recognize how
temporal blessing is in part a revealment of alienation,
how the oneness of lives with their source is achieved
not only through affirmation but also through denial,
through sacrifice, even loss of life.

But the doubleness in Hopkins' imagery differs, too,
from the doubleness in Byron, who in some ways
predicts the post-Romantic vein as he echoes the pre-
Romantic vein, and the doubleness in Tennyson, Browning, Arnold, and Swinburne. Byron could apostrophize
the mighty ocean as "image of eternity" in *Childe Harold's Pilgrimage*, and then he could go as far as any
realist in showing the ocean's natural destructiveness
and terror in the shipwreck scenes of *Don Juan*. Tennyson can suggest the calm majesty of the deep as a
cosmic womb and grave in the *Idylls* and "Crossing the
Bar," and yet in "Ulysses," for instance, he can view
the ocean as an element to be conquered, as the temporal outside force upon and against which men must
strive. Browning, in *Fifine at the Fair*, delights in the

natural buoyancy of sea water, yet he comes to think of
this nature as foreign and briny. Arnold, more obviously than the others, moves back and forth between
two views: sometimes he declares the primacy of external nature and urges men to sink into its depths, or like
Tennyson he finds the ocean a comforting image of
consummation in death, of oneness in one Nature (at
the end of "Sohrab and Rustum," this ocean is a resolution to the unbearable strife of human existence); but as
often he can say of the "unplumb'd, salt, estranging
sea" that it is meaningless to men—this is the disillusioned view of "Dover Beach." Unlike these vacillating
poets, Hopkins combines the sea of life with the sea of
death. He takes cosmic nature to be at once fallen and a
source of grace, at once mortal and a mode of showing
forth the Immortal. So it is with every image in the
seascape and landscape. While in "The Deutschland"
water brings about death and destruction, and light
means supernatural life, still every concrete image in
Hopkins inspires two responses and is concretely double. Unlike Swinburne, Hopkins does not wish to define the larger life of the natural ocean by drowning
every other form of life in it, and neither is he so
mystical, so single-minded—or, indeed, so inclined to
heretical monism—as to counter Swinburne by making
the ocean of the immanent a mere devilish or quite
illusory foil to his light of the transcendent.[2]

[2] The monism of Swinburne makes the sea, again and again,
drown out and negate every other image. Even the effect of

Of course, the double and sometimes paradoxical quality of Hopkins' imagery is not only Victorian; it is, more basically, Christian and derives from the Christian doctrine of Incarnation, the combining of God and man, or of eternity and time. But Hopkins reacts against a kind of immanent monism, toward which the great Romantics tended, in the distinctly Victorian imagery of harsh if necessary light, of the terrible if necessary depths. It is, in effect, Victorian Catholic imagery.

The contrast between and ultimate parallel of fiery heights and watery deeps that "The Wreck of the Deutschland" makes are perhaps foreshadowed in "A Vision of the Mermaids," written and illustrated by the poet at eighteen under the influence of Keats, but revealing some images that might well be thought characteristic of later works: "spikes of light / Spear'd open lustrous gashes, crimson-white," and the mermaids

---

Swinburne's syntax is to substitute one term for another, with kaleidoscopic shifting and without much development of any specific image or thing. Sometimes Hopkins indulges in such effects, too, giving the impression that everything echoes everything else; but he is more likely to move from one aspect to another of a palpable object or person. The syntax in "The Deutschland" is often double, differing from that of the Augustans by using many more "a and b" constructions, often with alliteration—and constant apposition. Like his rhyme and rhythm, the syntax is Hopkins' meaning: he declares the yoking of divine and corrupt, the incarnate mystery of God in nature, by constant yoking of apparent opposites—just as he suggests the ineffable power of the divine by using a series of terms none of which can be at all adequate.

spread bright "sea-gull plumes." [3] This vision of rosy brilliant sky and "ponderous sea, / The miles profound of solid green" ends by ascribing to the mermaids a "sweet sadness" in their "dusk depths." There is a faint and almost sentimental qualifying of Romantic joy in the life of the sea. That faint sense of pain in the waters if not in the brilliant skies of his picture is intensified in "The Deutschland" and is to be echoed later in the partly parallel but less ambitious "Loss of the Eurydice." Here the "blue March day" whose "bright sun lanced fire in the heavenly bay" is called a "liar," for the sky has soon gone dark with storm, and the training ship Eurydice, off the English coast, has suddenly capsized in "sea-swill," "Death teeming in by her portholes." Sky and sea are double and can be treacherous as well as benevolent. The poet's reflections upon this storm and shipwreck finally make a metaphor of the event: England in his generation is "fast foundering" in a sea of heresy and faithlessness. But within the metaphorical last section there is promise, too, in the memory of a time when for England the milky way was "Walsingham Way" pointing to Mary's shrine; there is hope if men will only "to Christ lord of thunder / Crouch," accepting with faith what the elements deliver. Man's response is the key to what natural events mean, whether grace or mere destruction. He may be

[3] J. Hillis Miller in *The Disappearance of God* (Cambridge, Mass., 1963), p. 275, suggests the influence here of Hopkins' Oxford tutor Walter Pater.

called upon to recognize God's purity in bright natural forms, as in "The Sea and the Skylark," where both the bird's song and the roar of the ocean "shame this shallow and frail town," "being pure!" [4] Or he may be called upon to accept shipwreck and thus find it an even greater means of grace. The sky is beautiful; from it come thunder and lightning. The sea is pure and magnificent; in it men drown. Yet thunder and drowning can be gifts. Behind all doubleness is one Power.

But no other long poem by Hopkins approaches "The Wreck of the Deutschland" for sustained and peculiar expression of the poet's inscape or for deeply and quite consciously ambivalent response to the nature of seascape.

The movement of "The Deutschland" is not only one from the personal present ("Thou mastering me,"

[4] The almost Wordsworthian conclusion, yet more bitter than Wordsworth's in "The World is Too Much With Us," declares that we

Have lost that cheer and charm of earth's past prime:
Our make and making break, are breaking, down

To man's last dust, drain fast towards man's first slime. The fascinating echo of "prime" and slime" suggests two opposed senses of the primeval: the pre-Adamic unfallen nature in which man was perfectly at home, and the nature of fallen man outside Eden, at the beginning of history. Surely "last dust," the merely mortal creature, equals "first slime," the creature who becomes slimy—and mortal—by his original sin. It seems curious, yet is characteristic of Hopkins, that no mention is made of the fallen mortal state of the landscape, the world of sea and skylark.

"I feel thy finger") to the narrative past ("On Saturday
sailed from Bremen" "Two hundred souls in the
round") to the optative, yearning toward a general
future ("Our King back, oh, upon English souls!"); it
is also one from light to light-drowning darkness to
light, from heaven to ocean to heaven, from glory to
suffering to glory. The imagery of fire flashing from
heaven, at the beginning and the end, is necessarily
metaphorical, the individual and imperfect expression
of a personal faith and a general hope. The imagery of
the narrative middle is that of an actual scene. The poet
describes no Coleridgean or Arnoldian sea, not an allegorical or metaphorical vision, but the terribly real
thing. And yet, if Hopkins is like Byron in recognizing
the horrors of this real sea, he does share with Arnold,
Tennyson, and even Swinburne the need to recognize
much more in the deep than temporary delight or
danger. For Hopkins, then, sea nature must be at once
real and symbolic.

   This poem about real and terrible nature, red indeed
in tooth and claw but also impersonally destructive,
addresses a personal God in its first word, *Thou*, and its
last, *Lord*. The poet's two ways of apprehending God,
as all-powerful master and as loving savior, are both
suggested in the first stanza, but the emphasis now is
upon power, upon a force to which man must say yes.[5]

   [5] Often, as here, Hopkins presents this pressure of God
which, when responded to, becomes instress, by tactile imagery:
"and dost thou touch me afresh? / Over again I feel thy

I did say yes
O at lightning and lashed rod;
Thou heardst me truer than tongue confess
Thy terror, O Christ, O god.

God is "lightning and love," "a winter and warm"; but the lightning and the cold come first. They pose questions, inevitably, for the religious poet. And this work can be read as a religious answer to just the questions about fierce physical nature—about lightning, cold, destructiveness— and about human mortality that Tennyson asks explicitly with *In Memoriam*. It is about the relation between the suffering self and the destructive sea of nature. It seeks to find the ground of that relation in Christ, Who is Self in self and more than self, and Nature in nature and more than nature.

Again, this is a poem about self in a specific literal way.[6] Stanzas two and three describe the speaker's own

---

finger." Geoffrey Hartman's chapter on Hopkins in *The Unmediated Vision* (New Haven, 1954) is a perceptive account of how important both tactile pressure, literal physical force of stress, and the resilience of self are in all of his poetry.

[6] John Pick observes that the poet is virtually identified with the nun, his heroine, because "in a manner he becomes Christ, and Paul and Austin and the nun are all participating in the life of Christ and reenacting the sacrifice of the Cross." He goes on to argue that Hopkins's reaction to the *Spiritual Exercises* of Ignatius Loyola is represented here, and, specifically, Hopkins' struggle before deciding to become a Jesuit. See *Gerard Manley Hopkins, Priest and Poet* (London, 1942), pp. 42–43.

suffering in the imagery of a buffeted bird, very much like "The Windhover," and of fire: his "dovewinged" heart can "flash from the flame to the flame," from divine displeasure to the threat of Hell (both forms of grace) and fly at last to the Host, the communion wafer of the sacrament. Hopkins' imagery shifts in the fourth stanza, where he is no longer "bold to boast": now "I am soft sift / In an hourglass" and "water in a well." But, like the bird, the sand and water have selves, are formed by "a pressure, a principle, Christ's gift." The very stress man suffers forms himself; and this reflection is as much a matter of self-analysis as of theology.

The water imagery may remind us that man's nature shares in the substance of the external nature which can drown him. That nature is seen now not in its brightness—"I kiss my hand / To the stars," declares the poet of God's grandeur, both saluting and for the moment dismissing nature in its beautiful aspect—but as an agent of stress, "Since, tho' he is under the world's splendour and wonder, / His mystery must be instressed, stressed." Stress is associated not with heavenly light but with waters and the dark. The necessity for men to be peculiarly stressed dates from the historical moment of the Incarnation; the poem declares that men have to imitate Christ, who is both immortal self and temporal victim, by accepting stress in order to receive full self-hood and a new life. Christ's coming into nature, then, His entering history, has brought a new kind of death into the world as the means to fuller life.[7] This death under stress is the fruit of the Incarnation, the sour sweet fruit of the eighth stanza, which leads men to emulate and adore the "hero of Calvary." But man cannot emulate alone; he has to be tired, his willful self sacrificed. The point is stated in stanzas nine and ten, which are reminiscent of the metaphysical poets, and more, perhaps, of the violent Donne than of Hopkins' favorite Herbert:

> Be adored among men,
>   God, three-numbered form;
> Wring thy rebel, dogged in den,
>   Man's malice, with wrecking and storm.

Like the Donne who cries out, "Batter my heart, three person'd God," the speaker looks for grace in discipline, declaring "[Thou] hast thy dark descending and most art merciful then." Remarkably, the very poet whose verse is more filled with joy in light than any other among the Victorians can now invite the darkness —and the terror—that the second part of this poem is to describe. In fact, as the tenth stanza (and end of the first part) asserts, the darkness is a mode of light: St. Paul was blinded by light, and his darkness was a sign of divine favor. The phrase "dark descending" is succeeded by the lines, "With fire in him forge thy will," "melt him but master him still." And at the end of this

---

[7] The theme is developed by T. S. Eliot in his dramatic monologue "The Journey of the Magi."

introductory section to a poem about a wreck there is neither mere personal resignation nor a more general lament of man's fate, but instead a communal hymnlike strain of prayer and praise:

> Make mercy in all of us, out of us all
> Mastery, but be adored, but be adored King.

These lines predict and are to be echoed in the last lines of the poem.

The second part begins with the words of a personified Death, who can use "flame / Fang, or flood," and it continues, still in the first person plural, to introduce the seasonal imagery Hopkins is to use elsewhere:

> We dream we rooted in earth—Dust!
> Flesh falls within sight of us, we, though our flower
>   the same,
> Wave with the meadow, forget that there must
> The sour scythe cringe, and the blear share come.

But this is not the main imagery of the poem. There is a nervous effect of sudden shifting from rhetorical device to metaphor to narrative images as, in stanza twelve, we are plunged into the story. And even then, after half a dozen short lines, the poet interpolates a question to re-emphasize the point of the first ten stanzas, that the unguessed fate of the "fourth . . . to be drowned" can be a grace:

> Yet did the dark side of the bay of thy blessing
> Not vault them, the millions of rounds of thy mercy not
>   reeve even them in?

Thus reminded, we proceed with two brilliant stanzas, both narrative and descriptive, introducing a scene that can be compared with the wild seascapes of Turner—perhaps with the famous "slave ship" painting ("Slaves Throwing Overboard the Dead and Dying—Typhon Coming On") and with Ruskin's vivid description of that picture.[8] In Hopkins's ocean scene "The infinite air is unkind"—here is one aspect of the element that in its other is to be called Marian, filtering the sun kindly—and the "deeps" are "widow-making unchilding unfathering." These brief grim comments on the stormy scene do not so much break into it as they intensify its point with their bleak language and rough rhythms. They belong with the exact description of how breakers smash the ship in stanza fourteen, a passage as close to Old English as any in Hopkins.

> And canvas and compass, the whorl and the wheel
> Idle for ever to waft her or wind her with, these she
> endured.

Yet another shift in method occurs in stanza fifteen, with a more curious effect. Again, there is personification, now developed in lines of rather Shelleyan allegory:

> Hope had grown grey hairs,
> Hope had mourning on,

[8] The comparison has been suggested by Alison Sulloway, of Beloit College, whose Columbia University dissertation deals with the influence of John Ruskin on the poetry of Hopkins.

But the literal sequence of events continues with stanza sixteen, about the brave sailor who is "pitched to his death at a blow," his body dangling for hours in the "cobbled foam-fleece," "the burl of the fountains of air." It reaches a climax after a terrible passage about the crushing storm and drowning waves that is at the same time a Turneresque and brilliantly exuberant passage describing the "sea-romp over the wreck": from the scene of sea life and men's deaths rises a human figure to transcend sea nature and her own mortality.

A lioness arose breasting the babble,
A prophetess towered in the tumult, a virginal tongue told.

Here, at the end of stanza seventeen, is a turning point. The heroic nun will, like the poet's heart in stanza three, "tower" above the tumult by seeking the heart of the Host. The poetic speaker, in what seems a natural development for the religious lyric, responds to her towering figure with the exclamatory rhetoric of the eighteenth stanza. For now his heart ("mother of being") has been "touched" in his body, his "bower of bone," and has been "turned for an exquisite smart," as, already in the first stanza of the poem with its parallel questioning rhetoric and tactile imagery, he has felt and been altered by the smarting "touch" of God. This heart of the speaker may be in part fallen, "unteachably after evil," but it can utter truth and so bring tears that are both like "melting" and like the beginning of music —the beginning, it seems, of a "glee," a song about "never-eldering revel and river of youth." The "madrigal start" may also mean a sudden, startled response, the tears for a heroine's courage that are more joyful, more musical, more gleeful than sad. But the essential burden of the stanza is that the goodness within the speaker's own soul is moved by a pang of joyous recognition, upon contemplating Christian courage, so that it can commence a poetic song (both glees and madrigals are songs, and song of course traditionally means poetry) upon the subject.

This madrigal for the nun, which is to become a hymn of praise and finally a prayer, begins with stanza nineteen. It seems in one sense literally a madrigal, a lyric suitable for music, in its rhythm:

> Sister, a sister calling
> A master, her master and mine!

In another more fanciful sense, this part of "The Deutschland," from stanza nineteen to the end, is like a madrigal because it includes several melodic lines or voices: the voice of the nun herself calling, the voice of the lyric poet which becomes at one point, under stress, a stuttering voice almost incapable of utterance, and the solemn voice of the hymn, recurring now and then and finally dominant. The harsh sea of dangerous nature is heard through all voices, and in these lines it is always present:

> The inboard seas run swirling and hawling;
> The rash smart sloggering brine
> Blinds her.

But, as it is for the poet's heart in the preceding stanza, salt "smart" can be "exquisite"; and the physically blinded "sees one thing, one." "She rears herself to divine / Ears," and her voice is louder than that of the storm.

Unfortunately, perhaps, the technique of shifting voice and focus, of joining personal reflection with narrative, allows the poet an animadversion that can be read as a falling-off, in stanza twenty, with its contrast of Saint Gertrude and Martin Luther. But if its music has been jarred, the poem again becomes both actual and intense in stanza twenty-one. The storm at sea is not quite forgotten as the poet associates his indoor stress with the different sufferings of his heroine. "Surf, snow, river and earth / Gnashed." Neither is the power forgotten, represented by the images of heavenly light that transforms tempests:

> Thou art above, thou Orion of light;
> Thy unchancelling poising palms were weighing the
> worth,
> Thou martyr-master: in thy sight
> Storm flakes were scroll-leaved flowers, lily-showers
> —sweet
> heaven was astrew in them.

The language would be sentimental were it not for the firm and grim sense of real storm, darkness, and death already established.

From this point on, however, the poem is again reflective rather than descriptive. The imagery of sea and shipwreck is like a ground tone set to be played upon, and in a sense transmuted, without being lost or denied. In the twenty-second stanza Hopkins lets himself improvise upon the number of the shipwrecked nuns, five, to associate it with the number of Christ's wounds.[9] To this association based on number is added, in stanza twenty-three, a reference to Saint Francis of Assisi, appropriate both because he visibly received the stigmata, the five wounds of Christ, and because the lost

[9] He is led by that association to declare that the number five signifies sacrifice (we must note, then, that the number five is that of "man's make," of man's essential style, or the way he is made, which is to be revealed only in self-sacrifice) and that the number is appropriately marked or scored (and "scores" can also mean cuts or stripes with a whip) in scarlet, in blood that symbolizes both a wound and life itself. That Christ marks his own, his chosen, by the bloody stigma of suffering imposed upon them is a religious commonplace—the good are hard and tried, saints must suffer—and also here is an echo of the idea earlier explained, of stress that, responded to, is instress—the "scoring" or scourging of men is another instance of physical stress, of natural impact as a form of divine grace. It is parallel to the lettering with red dye of the chosen lamb, for every Christian has to act in some degree, imitating the *Agnus Dei*, as a sacrificial lamb. At the end of the stanza this stress of scarlet is represented by an echo of the "storm flakes" in the stanza preceding (which become again in twenty-four the literal "thickly / Falling flakes" of snow) as the divine stress becomes a "ruddying of the rose-flakes": nature is colored and made beautiful, just as snowflakes can be transformed into flowers, only by a divinely directed force that also bloodies the bodies of martyrs.

nuns were Franciscans.[10] All of this is fanciful reflection and commentary upon the subject; it is personal, original, in style if not in matter.

With stanza twenty-four, the poet explicitly shifts back once more to himself, where he was when the shipwreck was happening: "On a pastoral forehead of Wales, / I was under a roof here, I was at rest." There is a contrast; but, by implication, there is once more a deeper parallel. The poet who speaks of himself in the first five stanzas and to himself in stanza eighteen, who refers in stanza nineteen to "her master and mine," is very close in his rest to those who are "prey of the gales." *Rest* rhymes with *best*, as the nun in the black air and falling flakes calls out to Christ and so "christens her wild-worst Best." Naming Christ in this worst moment makes it her best moment; like the speaker, she is "under a roof" (in "the dark side of the bay of thy blessing," according to stanza twelve), under the protection of God and most in his grace.

[10] Hopkins' phrase "lovescape crucified" is especially striking: it suggests not only the fivefold pattern of wounds, but also the inscape of Christ which is the very shape of love. And the seal, the sign or mark, of Christ's triumph, is now imprinted not only on the saint but also on those five nuns who reflect such credit on both Francis and Christ, "sisterly sealed in wild waters, / To bathe in his fall-gold mercies, to breathe in his all-fire glances." Drowned and saved, beyond drowning, they bathe not in water but rather in golden light ("fall-gold" may be both the intense yellow color of autumn foliage and the light that falls from heaven); they breathe not air but rather divine fire.

The passage beginning with stanza twenty-five is difficult partly because it is so tensely and intensely the poet's own. It brings entirely into the speaker's passionate contemplation all the elements of this poem: the dramatic moment of the nun's cry on the foundering deck, the scriptural and dogmatic background which is taken to give that moment its meaning, and the poet's hardly disguised feelings of stress, of frustration, and of aspiration. Here is one of Hopkins' most vivid confrontations of self and nature, appealing characteristically to the supernatural source of both. That source is expressed in the Word, *Christ,* the word uttered by his heroine. So he exclaims, "The Majesty!" commenting on the grandeur of the nun's own exclamation, and then asks what that exclamation means, to her and to him.[11]

[11] The echoing phrases, "Breathe, arch and original Breath," "Breathe, body of lovely Death," may perplex although they seem to mean that the nun's cry to Christ is "arch" in the sense of being original, sheerly her own response and thus a perfect expression under stress of her own style, her soul, her inscape; and that the mortal body uttering this cry is, at the point of death, most brave, most lovely, and—again—most itself. The rest of the stanza requires understanding a biblical allusion. Hopkins' heroine is contrasted with the sailors in the New Testament who supposedly called Jesus, "We are perishing," during a storm on Lake Gennesareth. (The poet is not quoting directly, but he has Matthew 14:23–33 in mind, a passage in which Simon Peter appears less steadfast in faith than he is to seem in stanza twenty-nine.) Unlike them, she looks to life, not death. And yet, like them, she looks to Christ and is to be saved by Him. Still, there remains the question of what she means and in what sense she calls to Christ: is she,

The answer to that question begins with the twenty-sixth stanza, which asserts that the martyr's heaven is beyond any earthly sensuous vision. The imagery is that of God's grandeur in nature, with all its glowing, brilliant light. But this imagery is inadequate to suggest the heaven beyond, to measure what eyes cannot see or ears hope to hear. The nature poet who has kissed his hand to starlight and the "dappled-with-damson west" begins his twenty-seventh stanza with a clear stern "No." "No, but it was not these"—not earthly reward or even an idea of heaven that earthly images imply. Clearly, again, the poet's subject is not insight into beauty but instress under pain, and the terrible grandeur imagined here is not immanent in creation but transcendent. Though earth may hint of heaven, heaven is never to be concevied of as the gaining of beauty—or as an escape from earthly pain. This difficult stanza means also that men are more likely to ask for relief from daily boredom and frustration, "The jading and jar of the cart, / Time's tasking," than from moments of stress, "danger, electrical horror." (Omitting "it is" before "fathers" will clarify the syntax.) And if every-day living "fathers" the desire for peace, for ease to the "sodden-with-its-sorrowing heart," this desire is carried a step "further" in private prayer and meditation as Christ's passion, according perhaps to the

---

so different from the biblical fisherman, "keen" in her sharp (keen) pains to achieve a Christian martyr's crown? The answer is No.

directions of Ignatius Loyola. With these lines, the Jesuit poet has once more introduced his own contrasting and parallel experience into the account of his nun; for, although the speaker's "sodden" heart has escaped to Christ in quiet prayer, the woman under stress is certainly neither depressed nor engaged in "prayer apart." "Other, I gather, in measure her mind's / Burden, in wind's burly and beat of endragonèd seas." Her cry is not for escape into peace, into springtime's "jay-blue heavens," but for the climax and consummation of instress, for a virtually mystical oneness of her resilient soul with the divine power forming, stressing, all but crushing it.[12] Inscaped selves are various, and each is unique; nature is variously bright and dark, inspiring and distressing; the ground for both is single, the Word words cannot speak, "*Ipse*, the only one, Christ."

The brave nun's heart seems "right" and her eye "single" because she fixes on and sees the One reality, barely expressed in this one word "Christ," that gives shape and coherence to an otherwise shapeless scene

---

[12] The approximating of this union, even the expressing of this desire, must be beyond the power of words to convey, as all mystics have affirmed. So the twenty-eighth stanza stutters and lacks adequate words. (I cannot agree with Gardner that the rhetoric has anything to do with "the frantic efforts of the drowning to save themselves"—see his *Study* (London, 1958) I, 62—or that the effect is one of hysteria.) There is only one word to express her desire, and this same word with all its variants, "Master," "King, Head," can never be enough to embody it.

and by implication to an otherwise meaningless world of nature. The odd third line in stanza twenty-nine, possibly the oddest in this poem, means that she has read that word in a seemingly unspeakable, incomprehensible night of shock. But the key adjective suggests much more than the meaning of the inexpressible, for "unshapeable" reminds us of a range of Hopkins' favorite terms and of his interest in "scape" or "shape," in "landscape," "seascape," "inscape," "lovescape." That faith which Ruskin once had in a divine shaping power inherent in nature, so that every view rightly seen composed itself into a landscape the artist should not try to re-compose, becomes for Hopkins a faith in the shapeliness, the continual ordering, of nature through Christ. The physical world of land and sea is multiple and yet coherent, has resilient parts that are ordered, bound, and held together by the stress of a unifying power; and this power is the incarnate Christ, without Whom there could be no landscape, no seascape, no inscape. All of this the nun sees and expresses by naming the Logos that forms all temporal shapes—"him that present and past, / Heaven and earth are word of, worded by." [13]

[13] So she echoes Simon Peter's declaration (in Matthew 16:16), "Thou art the Christ, the Son of the living God," and in this faith she is, as Peter was, a rock. She is as firm in the trying storm as the Tarpeian rock—and that reference to the Roman place of execution, in conjunction with Peter, the rock, reminds us that her steadfastness is associated with her imminent death—even though, in a sudden shift to a more immediately familiar image, her "beacon of light" is "blown" by

"Christ" is a word, a title, rather than a name. But stanza thirty begins with the holy name itself. Here the poem sounds less like a passionate entrance into the drama of stress than like a formal celebration of its result. Jesus becomes the "heart's light" that has illuminated His daughter, kindling her "beacon of light": He appears in this maid His daughter, and has glory in her action, as He first appeared incarnate in the maid His Mother.[14] Just as St. Anne is said to have conceived Mary in purity, and Mary in turn to have conceived Jesus without taint, so in a lesser way the virgin nun can be said to have conceived Christ, in her heart and brain, through the "Word, that heard and kept thee and uttered thee outright." These lines may indicate that Hopkins' insistence on the palpable inscapes of words is closely related to the idea, in Logos theology, of the creating word as the very sound and image of divine life. The nun's uttering of the word "Christ" has been an act of creation.[15]

---

the blast. The imagery, then, at the end of this densely packed stanza on the shaping word, plays upon words in a way that is both condensed and seriously witty.

[14] The poet can only ask (and often his syntax for ultimate matters is one not of saying but of asking) what the heavenly celebration of this nun's triumph has been. He links that celebration with the feast of the Immaculate Conception of Mary—a feast day that actually came immediately after the day of his heroine's death—and so he specifically associates the German nun with the Virgin.

[15] It can also have been an act of saving efficacy for others. The poet does not, after all, pass over those less than heroic souls who perished on the *Deutschland*. He can pity, his heart

The final four stanzas, making up one last and
hymn-like supplication, unite the passionately personal
and the formal or mythic-dogmatic aspects of this
poem. They also unite the two kinds of imagery that
have run through it and have helped, more than the
various and occasional images of sand and rock, of
meadow and harvest, to give it continuity. In them God
is both Orion of light and "master of the tides" (master
of Noah's flood and of every "year's fall," the autumnal
darkness in this fallen natural world of seasons). In
stanzas thirty-two and thirty-three the water imagery is
dominant. God is hymned as enclosing and quenching
the oceanic nature in its flux; He is the strand and floor
of waters, the principle that "bides" in natural forms

---

can bleed for, those who died unconfessed. But they may not,
in fact, have died uncomforted. Within the physical stress of
the storm, the brave sister has felt a more delicate, exquisite
touch, for now as in the first stanza of the poem God's most
personal and effective stress upon man is a mere but all-
important touch of His finger; and if she could respond to
that subtle Providence so fully, perhaps the others will have
responded as well, have been comforted and confirmed, by
her loud cry of faith and hope, her voice that is like a ringing
bell to call back stray sheep. The imagery changes now from
tactile to pastoral to yet another kind, anticipating Hopkins'
verse about seasonal nature, as the poet asks,

            is the shipwreck then a harvest,
        does tempest carry the grain for thee?

The question, with its positive implication for men in general
as well as the heroic soul, leads up to the last stanzas of praise
and prayer.

and also "bodes," gives signs and commands.[16] But the final imagery, that of the last two stanzas, does at last quite definitely transcend "the all of water." Strange as the comparison may seem, Hopkins uses water imagery as Milton does in "Lycidas," to give an associative coherence to several elements in his poem, literal setting, biblical reference, and the metaphor of divine power. Both poets finally rise above the imagery and all its purely temporal meaning. Hopkins' most intense language for praising God is that of fire and light; and so he exclaims of Christ's manifestation in the faith of his daughter:

> Now burn, new born to the world,
> Doubled-naturèd name,
> The heaven-flung, heart-fleshed, maiden-furled
> Miracle-in-Mary-of-flame.

And this manifestation of double nature, divine and human, all-powerful and Christlike in humility, is further explained in language that predicts the iconogra-

[16] Controlling the seas and boding, God can provide against tempests an ark like Noah's in the flood. Or, as we have now been shown, his seeming to bode ill may really be boding well: His love "glides / Lower than death and the dark." Not only those who listen to and linger, waiting, for him, but also those apparently past hope of prayer, the criminal and the dying man, those in uttermost need, can "mark"—both perceive and, as in stanza twenty-two, themselves signify—the rising above His death and theirs of God triumphant in Christ. They are "fetched in the storm of his strides," as the nun in this poem has been fetched through grace working in sea and storm.

phy of "The Blessed Virgin Compared to the Air We Breathe," as it echoes the fire and light imagery in stanzas two, twenty-one, twenty-nine, and thirty:

Not a dooms-day dazzle in his coming or dark as he came;
    Kind, but royally reclaiming his own;
A released shower, let flash to the shire, not a lightning of
                    fire hard-hurled.

God may appear in the lovely lights of nature, in the lightning force of His power, and also in this special incarnation, being kind—both "loving" and "kindred," or made human.

Finally, the nun drowned off the shore of England is asked to intercede for English souls, for a new and general dawning, an Easter or re-birth of Christ the Word and Light:

Let him easter in us, be a dayspring to the dimness of us,
                    be a crimson-cresseted east,
More brightening her, rare-dear Britain, as his reign rolls.

The Christ revealed in one word spoken by the buffeted heroine of this poem should be "our heart's charity's hearth's fire," a light new-kindled within us. So a poem that begins with, and concludes with, references to God, in every stanza of which the last line rhymes with the first, ends as it has begun with a passage upon grace in fire, first "fire of stress" and now "our heart's . . . fire."

At the same time, the ending is very different from the beginning. The final lines praise divine power in the figure of Christ as savior, not that of God the Father as Master; Christ's presence is imagined as precisely "not a lightning," and so it is quite unlike God's "lightning and lashed rod" in the second stanza. We have observed that the subject is broadened, too, from "me" to "us." Grace in its aspect of stress has become grace in the form of hope revealed; the response to it now is not painful introspection but aspiration to general atonement or at-one-ness with the deity. The plot of the poem, as we have seen, leads from self to nature to "English souls." In fact, it follows a frequent tendency in Victorian literature. In this Victorian plot movement, a central figure—whether author or character— begins by brooding on himself, on his sense of uncertainty and his internal suffering; tries to break away from self-consciousness and enter literally or imaginatively into the natural and social world of hard work, strife, and human interaction; and hopes to end with some promise for the future of society, often represented in a happy marriage or in a birth. If the shifts from stage to stage are abrupt enough, this movement may constitute what has been called the Victorian "pattern of conversion." Or the last stage may be represented as an ideal not achieved. This over-all movement is approximated in *Sartor Resartus*, *In Memoriam*, *Great Expectations*, and *Middlemarch*. In "The Deutschland" its stages are not neatly set off, but they are present: reflection upon personal and inner stress; entering into the drama of people under natural stress;

hope for a birth, a re-birth that is to wed men, as it were, to God and thus brighten their futures—and the future of the whole society, which is England.

Between the intensely personal first part and the hopeful, hymnlike last part, a great deal of matter has been compressed. At best, the condensation of meaning in this poem is brilliant and overwhelmingly effective, for the lines have such vitality that one reading reveals much of the meaning, which resides in rhythm and sound as it does in statement and imagery. Although "The Deutschland" may now and then give difficulty with its ellipses, inversions of word order, archaic or special terms, and sudden shifts of image, none of these stylistic complexities appears to be a serious defect, or a defect that is not from another point of view much more a delight and a virtue. There is a problem of focus inherent in the poet's abrupt move from his spiritual experience to the description of a romping storm seen with a painter's eye, then back to himself in Wales, then to reflections on melancholy, stress, grace, and so on. And yet the very abruptness of the shifting, like the abruptness of the elliptical syntax, seems to be an inevitable quality of this poem that yokes self and drama, inner and outer, the picture of this world's dark ocean and the imagery of another world's lights. Although the poem is often in danger of breaking into parts, it can be said at last to achieve a remarkable degree of coherence.

The degree of coherence is less than perfect, perhaps, and the quality of the poem is less than consistently high, not because of stylistic oddity or because of the poet's failure to mark transitions and to compose according to a visible and conventional logic, but because Hopkins can hardly sustain his characteristic intensity in a work of even this intermediate length. And to no other English poet is intensity so essential. When his imagination fails, the flatness that results—as in stanzas fifteen and twenty—is all the more a blemish for the brilliance that surrounds it. Other poets can sustain flat passages that lead up to the heights, or can keep a fairly prosaic narrative going in verse. Hopkins can not. His genius is lyric, extreme, and condensing, and his finest, most fully achieved works of art, more satisfactory as wholes than "The Deutschland," are such lyrics as "The Windhover," "Spring and Fall," and "That Nature is a Heraclitean Fire."

But this is not at all to say that "The Deutschland" is a failure or lacks poetic passages of the highest order. Nor is it to deny the absolute importance of the poem for Hopkins himself, and for an understanding of his work. In "The Deutschland" he is dealing with the imagery and themes that other Victorian poets have dealt with, but unlike his contemporaries he is taking a whole view of these. His overcoming death and the shock it occasions is more satisfactory than Tennyson's in the last parts of *In Memoriam;* Hopkins' positive faith, by accounting more fully for suffering in the world, is firmer than Browning's in *The Ring and the Book;* and Hopkins' reconciliation of man and nature, through a force higher than each, is more assured than Arnold's stoical attempts to achieve that end. Furthermore, "The Deutschland" sets the themes and images, as it introduces the rhythms, that Hopkins is to use from this time on. The "dovewinged" heart that flees and flashes in the third stanza anticipates and helps to explain "The Windhover." The first stanza of the second part, seeing flowers and meadow soon to fall under the scythe, and the end of the thirty-first stanza with the harvest carried to heaven, point toward the seasonal imagery of a number of poems, including "Spring and Fall." The series of dazzling passages on light and fire, both natural and divine, introduces Hopkins' favorite imagery, which implies a complex theme and is to be expanded in many poems, reaching a climax in the "Heraclitean Fire."

If it is not always perfectly sustained, "The Wreck of the Deutschland" is still Hopkins' most ambitious, and in some respects his most comprehensive and therefore most important poem. It is both a recognizably Victorian poem and an original achievement.

3 "The Windhover"

While shipwrecks occur on the ocean, men sleep peacefully in their beds; and in other climes birds sing. These are parts and pieces of the pied world; the sibylline, ambiguous truth in "Spelt from Sibyl's Leaves" is that this life is one of "stained veined variety," where "two tell, each off the other." When Hopkins turns from the poetry of instress and sacrifice to that of inscape and joy in nature, he may seem to move into another world, but he does not. An early and very Victorian poem, "The Nightingale," for the most part a soliloquy, contrasts a maiden, who listens anxiously to the sound of the bird, with her lover, who washes "from on deck" in "the frothy deep"; but with a chilling intuition she thinks that "the music" of the bird's song "must be death."

> With not a thing to make me fear,
> A singing bird in morning clear
> To me was terrible to hear.

And the last word of the poem, so unlike any Romantic address to a nightingale, is "wreck."

The singing or flying bird is not usually "terrible" in the mature Hopkins. The bird is one of his favorite images in nature, certainly his favorite animal image, and he uses it in several ways. The poet who describes his own heart as "dovewinged" in "The Deutschland" apparently in his lines entitled "Peace" longs for the wood dove, the peace of God which passeth all understanding, and perhaps at the same time the Holy Ghost, pictured as a dove, which brings that comfort.[1] Still, on earth, the allegorical bird, appearing only in brief moments and leaving his plume Patience behind, brings duties as well as delight.

> And when Peace here does house
> He comes with work to do, he does not come to coo,
> He comes to brood and sit.

In general, Hopkins' birds, literal or symbolic, suggest something more than natural freedom, more than sheer joy in flight and song.

If there are exceptions to this general remark, they are fragments such as "The Woodlark" and the delightful lines beginning "Repeat that, repeat." The first of these provides a good instance of the poet's full use of sensory images, of his delight in color, sound, and movement. The bird's uttered response to flying over the sunlit landscape of wheat, poppies, furrows, and

---

[1] Compare the final imagery of "God's Grandeur," where "the Holy Ghost over the bent / World broods with warm breast and with ah! bright wings."

trees, in the white and blue sky, is his song of "a sweet
—a sweet—sweet—joy." So intense and pure is that
response, in fact, that these verses might be about the
woodlark in Eden. But they are fragmentary. (The
lines have been printed by Gardner with Fr. Bliss's
additions to fill in missing lines.) And so is the undated
song of the cuckoo, in which "Repeat that, repeat"
rhyms with "delightfully sweet" and echoes in sound
the echoing sense of the lines. These five lines end,
"The whole landscape flushes on a sudden at a sound."
Yet the whole landscape, in the rest of Hopkins' poetry,
is not an Eden, and the earthly echoes are often leaden:
"ruck and wrinkle, dropping dying, death's worst,
winding sheets, tombs and worms and tumbling to
decay." These distort and echo mockingly the heavenly
golden sound heard pure on earth only in Eden. So in
"Spring" although the thrush "Through the echoing
timber does so rinse and wring / The ear, it strikes like
lightning to hear him sing," the song and all the other
beauties of the season are taken to be "a strain of the
earth's sweet being in the beginning / In Eden
garden."

In yet other poems, the bird that sings and soars,
instead of praising God only by being joyfully what it
is, has work to do in a work-cursed fallen world. In
"The Sea and the Skylark" both the flight and the song
of the lark, conjoined in the phrase "I hear the lark
ascend," act like the sound of the ocean to "shame this
shallow and frail town," "being pure." Like the singing

of the thrush, these are reminders to worldly men of what they have lost and forget they have lost, the "cheer and charm of earth's past prime." Although the affective difference between Hopkins and Wordsworth in similar passages may not be great, it is important that Hopkins specifies a real Eden, a past prime that is definite and of this world, not an Eden in the individual life or an unearthly pre-existence; and by clear implication he points to an ultimate joy and life outside and not deep within the dulled creation.

The bird's movement and song can teach man to remember and to praise the creator to which they ascend. His 1865 poem beginning, "Let me be to thee as a circling bird," gives the poet's own aspiration the form of a bird's flight, and most importantly a bird's song. The flight is circling but centered, the song continuous but one, with a "changeless note," as the poet's own "dominant" note would be the one authentic major strain of love for God, "to call thee Love and Love." The poem is interesting in several respects. It contains at least some hints of spiritual autobiography in the lines about the poet's having tried "each pleasurable throat that sings." (Perhaps he is suggesting several academic subjects, along with music, drawing, and poetry.) And his poem contains more hints of spiritual autobiography in the lines about the poet's having found his music "in a common word," instead of any "other science"—secular knowledge—or "minor sweetness"—possibly the arts. The common word is "Love," the word that ends the poem. God, or Love, or Christ, the Word, is com-

mon in being flesh and in being available to all through
a sacrament; and a vocation of love is to define the
speaker's "range and state." But it seems interesting,
too, that all of this is put first in the visual imagery of a
bird's or bat's flight and then in the quite traditional
poetic imagery of the bird's song, suggesting the art of
poetry. Sometimes in Hopkins' imagination there is
clearly not the division of loyalties between priestly
and poetic vocations that some critics have supposed.

Man as an artist, expressing himself in musical style, is
the subject of a better-known poem that uses the bird as
a means of comparison, "Henry Purcell." With this
work we return to the question of selfhood; and if the
image of the self does function now, if the art which
expresses self does function, we turn our thoughts to
love of the creator, as the final lines suggest. The very
first line of "Henry Purcell" is one of Hopkins' most
difficult, perhaps one of his most perverse, condensa-
tions, which omits both the normal subjunctive auxil-
iary and the understood noun—"may" and "fate" or
"end"—while repeating almost everything else.[2] But
while the poem does not appear to be difficult after this
beginning, it is really richer in implication, more truly
condensed, from this point on. It does not only state a
nineteenth-century "expressive" theory of art.[3] It is

[2] For the first version of this poem see W. H. Gardner's
Study, (London, 1958) I, 101.

[3] But it *is* in part an example of what M. H. Abrams calls
the "expressive" or "Romantic" theory of art, in *The Mirror
and the Lamp* (New York, 1953).

about even more than art, style, and selfhood. It sums
up the idea of inscape without using that term and
suggests finally, if one reads the last line correctly, the
paradoxical ability of unique self—which might seem to
be isolated by uniqueness—to communicate itself and
its source. In considering the life of the musician, Hopkins rules out not only all that is dross, his being "listed
to a heresy," but also all the various and, so to speak,
accidental qualities of his music, its mood, the effects of
"proud fire or sacred fear, / Or love or pity," that it
might have in common with other music. He concen-
trates on individuality, "abrupt self," but on the individual style that "throngs the ear," that is heard by
others—as the sign of the sea bird is seen by others.
Hopkins means by inscape not mere individuality but
the active expressing of it; if there is an existential spirit
in his assertion that each self cries out, *"What I do is
me,"* then there is in the further assertion (of "As
kingfishers catch fire") that "Christ plays / Through
the features of men's faces," an essentially cognitive
theory of art and nature, and indeed a sacramental
theory. Purcell's "forged feature finds me," for in a
moment I truly know him through his music, and I also
know a form of Christ this way. The single white
plume or feather of a "great stormfowl" on the "sea-
beach" (the bird and the stormy sea are related again)
reveals his style and self to us, just as a person's smile
can at once be self-revealing. And this "meaning mo-
tion," this revelation, "fans fresh our wits with won-

der" because it is a revelation of the creator through the creature, of the changeless One in the unique one, of Christ in the image. In the first few lines of this poems's sestet, music is said to have "moonmarks" and "wings." And while the poem manages such smooth transition from music to the metaphor of a bird, and thus from art to nature, it also manages to imply at last a sacramental meaning in music and bird, in art and nature, in all expressions of self.

To be imaged, to be selved or shaped, grace must produce and then enter into and act upon tractable but fixed and limited beings, men, birds, and objects; and to be incarnate is of course to be caged in the flesh. One of Hopkins' most interesting poems about birds uses just this language to express the frustration and dullness of being incarnate along with the necessity of physical as well as spiritual individuation. "The Caged Skylark" also states the Catholic doctrine of the risen body, the belief that human forms after the Last Judgment and the resurrection of the dead will be perfected and will not be only the corruptible bodies of this life. But, more than exposition of doctrine, these lines are moving in their intensely personal sense of how dreary the physical self can become. Man's skylark spirit sometimes sings in his body, but sometimes wrings its "barriers in bursts of fear or rage." Finally, the poem contrasts man's spirit in the temporal world with the spirit released from physical life, one a caged skylark and the other a free wild bird. The blessed spirit, presumably after death and in heaven, still requires the home which is the body, but now its flesh is not like a cage so much as it is like a nest; the purged and risen spirit, although "flesh-bound," will not feel any more burdened than the free lark feels imprisoned in its natural home or the meadow feels pressed down by the rainbow that spans it. In fact, in the perfect state not now of Eden but of an afterlife, there will be no tension at all between inner reality and scape, between the self and the self's truest nature.

But Hopkins more often displays an interest in the actual, experienced relation between inscape and land-scape, and specifically between self and outer physical nature. In a fascinating and mysterious fragment dated 1866 and beginning, "The earth and heaven, so little known, / Are measured outwards from my breast," he seems to be concerned with the interaction of the fixed viewer, "the unchanging register of change," and such shifting phenomena as the swallow that "drops upon the wind." The fragment breaks off, "O lovely ease in change of place! / I have desired, desired to pass . . ." This may suggest an early Romantic wish to escape from self, to be one with the flying bird, the vapor, rain, and cloud—to escape as "The Caged Skylark" tells us man can only after death, and not then by being disembodied. At any rate, the mature poet is repeatedly to put it that Christ is the pattern and culmination of earthly selfhood and at the same time the link between subjectivity and objective reality. Hopkins' man who acts most freely, who is most true to his own nature, is most Christ-like; and what he perceives of the beauty in external nature is God's grandeur incarnate, that is, Christ.[4] For Hopkins, to be sure, neither the greatest saint nor the most glorious landscape is identical with Christ; but expressing self to others and perceiving the inscapes of things, indeed all genuine communications, are apparently possible only to the extent that the principle of Christ, of divine grace in the body, operates. So, one might say, in Hopkins' mind, every man is a vicar and every thing is sacramental. Because the bird seems to him, along with man, the most free and graceful of natural creatures, and because it is both distinct from man—a part of the ordinary landscape—and perceived by man's two senses of vision and hearing, Hop-

---

[4] This virtual identifying of inner and outer, subject and object, perceiver and perceived, makes a kind of Christian parallel to Wordsworth's early doctrine of the mind that both gives to and takes from the world of external forms. Yet there can never be for any man a perfect Christlike selfhood, and the nature in which God is imaged is still partly flawed. In his important essay "On Personality, Grace, and Free Will," Hopkins asserts that "a self is an absolute which stands to the absolute of God as the infinitesimal to the infinite. It is an infinitesimal in the scale of stress." And his editor comments that for Hopkins "there are a series of 'pitches,' " corresponding to the critical moments in a man's life, by which he ascends or fails to ascend to the complete personality that God has destined for him." This complete personality would be the most nearly Christlike he could achieve. See *The Sermons and Devotional Writings of Gerard Manley Hopkins*, ed. Christopher Devlin, S.J. (London, 1959), pp. 153, 339.

kins often uses this attractive image to represent the free action of man's spirit and the sacramental meaning of nature. Often the bird represents both at once.

Hopkins' "Windhover" has something in common with his other birds: with the nightingale, an omen of destructive forces in nature; with the dove, a sign of perfect peace; with the woodlark, a source of joy in God's grandeur; and with the cuckoo, an image of natural beauty; with the thrush and the skylark, which, like the creatures Adam saw and heard, suggest pure Edenic nature; with the bird whose single strain is love of God; with the stormfowl, the unique self; and with the caged lark, the human spirit; even with the free flying bird that constantly moves and changes. Divergent as interpretations of "The Windhover" have been, and the poem has been explicated more variously than any other of comparable brevity in English, most commentators agree that the bird itself has at least three meanings: it is a real windhover, it represents Christ, and it comes to represent as well the man who would imitate Christ, possibly the poet himself. Another, not contradictory, way of putting it is that the bird is a real one merging into a symbol for all of nature, is a bird of omen that by reminding the viewer of Christ's life predicts the Christian's life, and, as it joins physical nature and the divine nature of Christ, is an image of the human self. It acts simultaneously as all of these.

This creature suggests beauty and joy within the creation, as the cuckoo, thrush, and skylark do, but goes beyond these by suggesting as well that the creation has become fallen and faltering since Eden, subject to having its pride, beauty, and very life bent, or even broken.[5] The freely flying windhover, after all, has something essential in common with the sillion of a plowed field and the broken embers of a dying fire.

But the windhover reminds us as well of a moment in natural history that balances the fall from Eden and profoundly qualifies the sense in which all creature life must fall and gall itself, turning the very act of falling into a means of repairing the original fall. Beginning as a poem about the glory of God incarnate in the creature, so intense a glory as to intimate the Nativity of Christ, this becomes a poem about the sacrifice of natural beauty and pride, so phrased as to imply the Crucifixion of Christ, the archetypal breaking of creation and

[5] This point is probably the crucial one for interpreting the poem; what follows here is generally in agreement with all commentators who see the windhover as a Christlike image of self-sacrifice, and in disagreement with all those who see the bird as only a bird or as only an example of natural grandeur and vitality. One recent summing up of interpretations for the poem is that by F. X. Shea, S. J., "Another Look at 'The Windhover,'" in *Victorian Poetry*, II (1964), 219–239 which follows but expands upon John Pick's reading—with some further reference to Catholic thought—and also agrees with J.-G. Ritz's highly complex interpretation. See the (London) *Times Literary Supplement*, May 6, 1955. Father Shea's criticism of the readings given by Richards, Empson, and McLuhan is particularly acute.

of the Creator within creation.[6] And the last lines suggest that these events set a pattern of inborn virtue coming to accepted sacrifice, of Christmas leading to Good Friday and Easter, of inscape implying instress, for all of nature and especially for all men. More than the boding nightingale, the windhover becomes an omen, in fact a universal omen.

The bird is finally the human self, with fuller implications than the bird of a single note, which praises God in its lyric, or than the stormfowl in "Henry Purcell," with its single unmistakable style. But this is the point most subtle, most implicit, and most open to challenge. We had better now turn to a close reading of the poem to see if this assertion, along with the others, does emerge.

Like so many short verses by Wordsworth and Keats, the poem begins with "I." It is about a first-person experience. But while this form of pronoun does not recur, the form "my" appears three times. What is done at the first—"I caught"—is an act of perceiving, catching sight of the bird but also catching its meaning. The windhover is "morning's minion," a small creature beloved of the morning and also, perhaps, the royal favorite; this second meaning is reinforced by the next phrase, which makes the bird not only a favorite of its

---

[6] A very recent article goes so far as to argue that the poem "depicts the specific event of the Crucifixion." See George E. Montag, " 'The Windhover': Crucifixion and Redemption," *Victorian Poetry*, III (1965), 109–118.

sovereign, the morning, but the very crown prince of the daylight kingdom, and thus light is twice associated with royalty, as in "The Deutschland." There is at least a moment of ambiguity, too, when the line ends with "king-," and Hopkins deliberately breaks in the middle of his word, so that the dauphin or prince himself appears, at first, to be the ruler—as Christ is both Son of God the Father and Christ the King. The falcon is, then, favorite of morning, prince of daylight, and also "dapple-dawn-drawn," attracted, as well as outlined and thus described, by the dappled or unevenly spotted clouds in the first rays of the sun. To "catch" the bird is to perceive all this quality. But to catch him fully is to perceive more, is to see the creature in flight, "in his riding."

He rides the "rolling level underneath him steady air"; reading that all but breathless combination of modifiers, so that we have a sense of a single reality with various simultaneous aspects, we may fail to notice that these aspects, especially "rolling" and "level," seem to contradict one another. Even assuming that the air rolls in a regular or level current, and remembering that air means life's matrix in "The Blessed Virgin Compared to the Air We Breathe," a reader cannot escape the odd sense of doubleness, of sustaining nature constantly in flux. The windhover, like the swallow dropping in the wind in Hopkins' lines, "The earth and heaven, so little known," exists in an element where all things "stir and range," "whirl or dive or fly," and yet an element of permanent impermanence, of level rolling and steady surprise. The ecstatic bird strides, like a justly proud man, and rides "upon the rein of a wimpling wing," curving and fluttering his wings even while he makes a regular are like that made by a horse turning on his rein; again there is free rolling movement within a clear linear pattern. And "then" he swings into another curving pattern: we imagine the shift from ascending flight in an arc, with curling to a gliding swoop, wings steady, describing a bow in the sky as a skate's heel would on ice. We can even take it that the first movement is "hurl" and the second "gliding," both of them rebuffing "the big wind," triumphing over the elements. But our moods and fates change with the elements and there is no perfect steadiness in this air: the wind rebuffed and mastered may rebuff and dash a proud creature, as the storm winds of "The Deutschland" do. The "heart in hiding" has "stirred for a bird" and has delighted in the sheer virtue of the creature, and the physical "mastery of the thing" ("thing" may be the act, or the bird, or the air mastered, any or all thought of impersonally). But this emotion of delight in nature may be changed, as it is abruptly after the octave.

The argument for this change in the poem can be based not only on a reading of the key word "buckle," so much debated, but also on the development of tenses and on the meaning and relevence of the last three lines in "The Windhover." The poem has three terms that act as time qualifiers, "this morning," "then," and once

more "then," marking the speaker's first view of the
bird, the bird's shift from wing-fluttering flight to gliding, and the moment when "fire breaks from thee,"
"my chevalier"; but the shift in actual tense of the
relatively few verbs changes this sense of normal
progression in time. The verbs in the first six lines,
"caught," "rung," "rebuffed," "stirred," are in the past
tense. The one verb in the next three-line section,
"buckle," must be in the present tense whether it is read
as an imperative or as an ordinary verb making a statement (all these things do buckle here). And the verbs in
the last lines, "makes," "fall," "gall," and "gash," are
also clearly in the present tense. The first section, the
octave, is about what was seen "this morning," the
second section is about what always is or can be at a
certain time, "then" (when something is done "here"),
and the third section is about what *is* generally true
with no qualification of time at all. These final three
lines, we shall have to conclude, describe how earth and
embers can generally be made to shine or show light by
being broken, by giving way to physical stress. The
proud masterly bird of the first lines must have something to do with such a giving way or breaking of
creature objects; he does only if we understand the
verb "buckle" to mean "bend" under stress. As there is
no logical transition from the first to the second section,
no such word as "but"—"but" is a word implicit in
virtually all Hopkins' poetry and a word virtually
never used in it—once more as with "The Deutsch-

land" we have to leap in mood from delight in natural power and ecstasy to moral reflection, from joy in inscape to a sense of instress.

Not that we are left without a relationship. The last word in line six is "thing" and the first in the next section is "brute," both deliberately unemotional ways of referring to a beautiful bird, of keeping it firmly within the realm of physical nature. And the nouns in the long series that makes up most of the seventh line clearly refer to qualities earlier ascribed to the wind-hover, even echoing the word "air," which now, however, means the bird's own air or manner as he masters his element of air. The real turn comes with the crucial verb that seems to reject our whole picture of bird and airscape: with a metaphysical effect of contradicting himself (which Hopkins uses again in the "Heraclitean Fire"), the eighth line begins by rounding off that series of nouns in the verb "buckle." Some commentators make this an imperative, a command to the bird or to the speaker himself (a reflexive imperative), telling one or the other to buckle on as a belt or armor all the qualities named, beauty, pride, and so on. Others take it as an indicative meaning that these qualities all "buckle" together and flash forth. But these meanings would not be very powerfully related to the end of the poem; they would take the bird in flight as only another more complex example of natural beauty, along with earth and ember. The verb could also mean something like "buckle to" or "buckle down"—to set to work, to apply one's energy. There is no indication of what the bird, or character, or speaker, might set to work at, unless one gives special emphasis to "plod" in the eighth line and reads the whole poem to mean a turning from the enjoyment of nature to dutiful plodding work; this may be an overtone consistent with the third meaning. But surely the main sense of "buckle" in the sequence of vision, reflection, and generalizing on nature, ending with the ploughed-down sillion and gashed embers, is to warp or bend under stress—and perhaps buckling down to dull work *is* giving way to the stress of duty —so that the windhover like the dovewinged heart of "The Deutschland" feels pressure that is instress. Its pride and air buckle, without utterly breaking, under this pressure, and "then" it can "flash" itself forth (just "as kingfishers catch fire," too):

> AND the fire that breaks from thee then, a billion
> Times told lovelier, more dangerous, O my chevalier!

The moment of the bird's buckling under the force of the wind has shown forth his grace, his inscape, in a flash, and so it has "told" the viewer, who before had caught his pride and power, of a much lovelier self —a fire that "breaks" forth, an inner light more brilliant than the outer daylight, and a more "dangerous" one. "Dangerous," the word Hopkins applies elsewhere to "mortal beauty," may carry the usual sense: the sacrificing or buckling of self under pressure of instress in this mortal world is indeed dangerous, for the bird might be dashed to death by stormy air as the brave sailor of "The Deutschland" was. It also has the Chaucerian senses of "haughty" and "supremely delicate." The highest air and purest pride consist in the ability to give onself up to the stress of God's power. In the final word of this short crucial section, "chevalier," some meaning of aristocratic hauteur may work, but also the meaning of a pride pure and high—the very opposite, indeed, of the sin called pride—that is the quality of Christ, who is also called Lord and who in religious adaptations of romance is represented as the knight, champion, or cavalier of all mankind. It is of course true that the bird itself has already been given some associations with horsemanship. He rides the air and like a horse or chevalier (horseman) he rings upon a rein. But the exclamation is so extraordinary, so reminiscent of personal addresses to Christ, that in connection with the poem's dedication "To Christ our Lord," which may indeed mean as much an address as it does a dedication, this phrase has made most readers suppose that the poet sees his Lord imaged in the figure of the bird.

The last three lines begin "No wonder of it," meaning surely that it is not wonderful but natural that brighter fire bursts from a creature buckled under stress than from one flying in its freedom, air, and pride. This conclusion repeats the message of stanzas five to eight in "The Deutschland," the message that since Christ's incarnation and crucifixion all of nature, and especially man, must follow the arch-pattern of self-revealing through self-sacrifice, of showing the highest inscape under instress. Earth, when plodded down by the ploughman, shines brilliantly; and from the ember, when it is broken, a fiery light breaks. These are extreme examples, and if stress produces such results from the very images of dullness, from clods and "blue-bleak" coals, then there is indeed no wonder that an already bright and lively thing should flash forth, should tell or show, under stress of the air, a light a billion times lovelier than its merely brute beauty.

In the next to the last line, the speaker addresses someone as "my dear," with a phrase perhaps more ambiguous than some more often debated. It can refer to the bird, or to Christ "my chevalier," or just possibly to the poet himself (although Hopkins does not seem elsewhere to use this Henry Jamesian form) or possibly to the reader, the imagined audience.[7] Perhaps it is not

---

[7] As Gardner points out in his fourth edition (p. 268), the phrase "Ah my dear," is used to address God by George Herbert in "Love" [2]. The fact may throw some doubt upon the rest of this paragraph. In any event, after the variety of interpretations that "The Windhover" has received, one has to recognize that the poem is to a great extent ambiguous—even if one insists, as this reading does, upon its coherent central meaning, that nature and man, imitating the pattern of Christ, are most beautiful and most themselves when they come under stress. (As Hopkins himself puts it, "The keener the consciousness the greater the pain; the greater the stress of being the greater the pain: both these show that the higher the nature the greater the penalty." See *Sermons and Devo-*

an "either-or" ambiguity, for it may address all at once.
But one might put special emphasis on this possibility,
for the poem ends as a comment on what has been
demonstrated, and a comment that hardly needs to be
made to either the bird or Christ. If this is so, the poet
might be directing his last remark to his dear reader, as
if to the dear auditor of a sermon, because the truth of
the remark applies directly to the reader. Implicit in the
nature of the bird is the nature of Christ which became
with His Incarnation the nature of nature, but most of
all, the nature of man.

And if this is so, finally, the poem is about the bird as
it represents the physical world of inscapes, mortal
selves; as it represents the pattern of Christ's coming,
sacrifice, and greater glory; and also as it represents the
necessary human pattern of sheer inscape and hard instress, of self-revealing and self-sacrifice. So the windhover is a real bird, the sign of Christ, and an omen
and teacher for men.

Hopkins' windhover in some ways resembles other
soaring birds in earlier nineteenth-century English poetry. It may remind us of Keats's nightingale and of
Shelley's skylark, for it is partly like the speaker himself
and yet, transcending his ordinary world in its splendor, it can inspire and teach him. But Victorian poets

---

tional Writings, p. 138.) The critical question is whether
ambiguity vitiates the poem, as Yvor Winters argues, or en-
riches its meaning by suggesting a number of reasonably
alternative and ultimately consistent possible meanings within
a framework of one coherent meaning.

are likely to find not only some strangeness and danger in the great Romantic images of mountains and seas but also sadness in the short lives of the creatures in a landscape. Swinburne's "Itylus," for instance, re-tells the ancient story of Philomela the nightingale and Procne the swallow, and so his essentially human nightingale is a victim, very different from Keats's immortal bird. Arnold's Philomela, too, sings of passion and pain. And Hardy, who has several verses on the ironic contrast between birds' singing and the world in which they sing, insists in "Shelley's Skylark" (a poem of 1887) that the real bird, distinct from the poet's image, is a "ball of feather and bone" that has perished as all natural things must perish. Hopkins' bird, like these, is a creature emblematic of the self, one subject to suffering, as well as an inspiring and transcendent image.

Like most of Hopkins' other birds, then, and indeed like most Victorian poetic images taken from the landscape, this creature has more than one positive meaning or function. It invites an ambivalent response, for it reveals the splendor of life in its pride, the living nature that should lead man to praise his Creator, and also the danger of wreck, the experience of buckling under stress, that should force man sacrificially to accept the will of his "martyr-master." The "I" whose heart is "in hiding" and the "dear" reader too must catch both meanings, knowing that the bird's flight in the air implies the stormy air's fierce wrecking of the creature, as inscape implies instress, and as spring in the fallen world implies the fall.

4 "Spring and Fall"

The seasons of the year become for many Victorian poets more than settings for mood or occasions for descriptive writing. Coleridge in "Frost at Midnight" and Keats in the ode to Autumn could make winter and fall display their beauties; but Tennyson finds death in summer's flowering; and Arnold repeatedly broods on how one season after another tries the human spirit with searing heat and bitter cold and finally kills it. *In Memoriam*, with its fourfold plot structure divided by the three Christmases and with its four-line stanza, attempts at last to foresee some distant apotheosis of mankind within time. The series of elegies, however, is always haunted by a sense of winter implicit in spring, of death remembered at the time of the Nativity, of four seasons that speak, each in its own way, or mortality and grief. Tennyson may fear, Browning observe, Arnold regret, and Swinburne exult that time conquers all: whatever the poet's response, this theme of the Triumph of Time is one both recurrent and profound for an age when most men have to seek within time the meaningful life that time seems to obliterate.

In Hopkins' dappled world there is almost never a living thing that does not show the seeds of its mortality, a springtime that does not at once predict both fall and winter. And so the mixed sense of life's joys is deeply felt in his poetry, more terribly than it is in that of Keats. If both "The Deutschland" and "The Windhover" can be read as sermon poems which finally accept and see beyond the stress of sacrifice demanded of natural bodies, it is nevertheless true that Hopkins' concern for the embodied life of landscape and man-shape remains too deep to be easily transcended. He does not lose his artist's love and need for mortal beauty, and it is no derogation of his faith in the supernatural that he yearns toward the natural as well.[1]

Neither Ruskin nor any other Victorian defender of the landscape against men's depredations has described more strikingly than Hopkins the liveliness of things, of birds, water, and trees. In a fragment about ash boughs he declares that nothing he sees "so sighs deep / Poetry" to his mind "as a tree whose boughs break in the sky." With agonizing knowledge almost put aside, Hopkins often delights in bits of landscape; the 1881

[1] In fact there is precedent for his emphasis on natural values in the work of his mentor John Henry Newman—and especially in *The Idea of a University* where, at the end of Discourse V defending the "temporal object" of "Knowledge its Own End," Newman declares, "We attain to heaven by using this world well, though it is to pass away; we perfect our nature, not by undoing it, but by adding to it what is more than nature, and directing it towards aims higher than its own."

lines "Inversnaid," in northern dialect, celebrate brown
falls and dark pool, asking:

> What would the world be, once bereft
> Of wet and of wildness? Let them be left,
> O let them be left, wildness and wet;
> Long live the weeds and the wilderness yet.

But the more familiar "Binsey Poplars" (1879) about
aspens whose cagelike limbs "quelled or quenched in
leaves the leaping sun" is also about their being
"felled."

> O if we but knew what we do
> When we delve or hew—
> Hack and rack the growing green!

Here, as later in the "Heraclitean Fire," he laments
man's insensitivity and destructiveness, the ease with
which beauty can be destroyed—as the eye can with a
prick be blinded—so that

> Ten or twelve, only ten or twelve
> Strokes of havoc unselve
> The sweet especial scene.

The inscape or "self" of the poplar, then, is easily blotted out. Like every form of landscape splendor, this
must, however painfully, be known as short-lived, as
mortal in itself. It may be "unselved" by man, or storm,
or fire. But he knows as well as Ruskin that waters are
often and easily polluted, that streams dry up, and in

any case that weeds and wilderness are not left, do not always live long—and may not be altogether good.

> Maidens shall weep at merry morn,
> And hedges break and lose the kine,
> And field-flowers make the fields forlorn,
> And noonday have a shallow shine,
> And barley turn to weed and wild.

These early (1865) lines are from "The Summer Malison," about a harsh season in the lives of men and women as well as of flowers and crops: in the dry tired land the mother's milk is dry, the father, the soldier, the sailor are tired and disillusioned, "and every heart thinks loathingly / Its dearest changed to bores." To this summer of sterility, in time, spring will give way.

And then comes winter. In a much later fragment that Gardner takes to be a sketch for "Spelt from Sibyl's Leaves," Hopkins gives the seasonal reference, together with his characteristic language about light and darkness, wreck, and impotence to work, an almost morbidly self-conscious sense:

> The times are nightfall, look, their light grows less;
> The times are winter, watch, a world undone:
> They waste, they wither worse; they as they run
> Or bring more or more blazon man's distress.
> And I not help. Nor word now of success:
> All is from wreck, here, there, to rescue one—
> Work which to see scarce so much as begun
> Makes welcome death, does dear forgetfulness.

To be sure, the spring and summer landscape, when not strictly earthly and not used to suggest the nature of earthly selves, need not grow so dark. A golden echo answers this leaden echo in the growing things and seasons that are metaphors of the heavenly, unchanging, non-temporal life. For Hopkins often finds the literal decaying body of time to be an image, faint or clear, of the ideas traditionally expressed in religious art by heavenly fruit, bread, trees, and so on, and by the days and seasons of the church calendar. Temporal images, again, like the dark ocean and the windhover, combine the several meanings: they are earthly things, and they are like sacramentals.[2]

The process works, and emphasis can go, both ways. When it does not, when sacramentals and icons lack earthly reality, they seem both brief and thin. In the two versions of the lines, "For a Picture of St. Dorothea" those miraculous fruits and flowers associated with the saint and martyr could not be from Caesar's gardens at this time of year, "because their buds not spring; / Spring not, for world is wintering"; and in fact they seem very soon to fade into the stars and "evening sky." The pun on "spring," opposed to "wintering," suggests that heaven's eternal spring appears only briefly in earth's bleak winter. And perhaps the miraculous appearances on this earth must quickly fade.

---

[2] A sacramental, as distinct from one of the sacraments, is a natural object not transformed but given special sacred meaning, as medals, holy water, and palm leaves may be.

There can be something of a clear (almost Pre-Raphaelite) literal-mindedness in Hopkins: it is not that he insists only on present realities, but that he does repeatedly insist on the reality, sometimes inspiring, sometimes frustrating, of the here-and-now. And he does so within the very poems that use the traditional iconography of a heavenly there-and-forever. His early lines "New Readings," in the manner of George Herbert, make the thorns around Christ's head into grape vines —as Christ's blood is the wine of the sacrament—the fruit of which produced "food for five thousand." But this is not a very characteristic work (except as it predicts in the line "CHRIST at all hazards fruit hath shewed" the poet's much later fear of being fruitless). And it never escapes into fancy at the expense of what is conceived as historical reality. Here is a real victim shedding, after all, real blood, and One who insisted on his being of the hard here and now when He "would not have that legion of winged things / Bear Him to heaven on easeful wings.[3]

In fact, the subject of heavenly fruitfulness is less frequent in Hopkins than that of spiritual sterility on earth. Often spring seems chill to him. In "See how

[3] Even more obviously inspired by George Herbert, probably, as Gardner's note hints, by Herbert's "The Bunch of Grapes," is "Barnflower and Winepress," a poem of 1865 about Christ the bread and wine, the fruit of the Tree, planted and flourishing in the form of the church. These merely competent lines are even less characteristic of Hopkins (as a mature poet) than "New Readings."

Spring opens with disabling cold," the literal cold of
English springs is the basis for a "chilling remem-
brance" of wasted, fruitless years; and these lines, so like
the terrible sonnets of his maturity, were written in the
poet's twenty-first year! (A poem produced a few
months afterward, "My prayers must meet a brazen
heaven," is even more like—is, indeed, astonishingly
like—the dark verse of twenty years later.) We can go
directly from them to the better-known ones of 1889
beginning "Thou art indeed just, Lord, if I contend,"
which end with a harsh self-judgment.[4]

> See, banks and brakes
> Now, leavèd how thick! lacèd they are again
> With fretty chervil, look, and fresh wind shakes
> Them; birds build—but not I build; no, but strain,
> Time's eunuch, and not breed one work that wakes.
> Mine, O thou lord of life, send my roots rain.

The sense in which the speaker is "time's eunuch" is the
sense in which, as a man, priest, and poet, he tries and
largely fails to achieve more than natural ends, more
than lies within the compass of time. But Hopkins often
sets the imagery of earthly, seasonal vegetation against
his feeling of incapacity. In lines for Robert Bridges
("To R. B."), he writes of his poetic power, his con-
ceiving mind, as requiring so long to mature—not nine

[4] Yet the poet puts himself on speaking terms with God,
addressing him as "sir"—as he does again in the lines beginning "Thee, God, I come from, to thee go," which end,
"Help me, sir, and so I will [pay my debt]."

months but nine years in which to recollect and form
life—that his creations lack "the roll, the rise, the carol"
of great art, and his is now only a "winter world." And
there is no more touching statement, although it does
not make a successful poem, than these fragmentary
lines about the extremely self-conscious, self-doubting
mood.

> Trees by their yield
> Are known, but I—
> My sap is sealed,
> My root is dry.
>
> If life within
> I none can shew
> (Except for sin),
> Nor fruit above,—
> It must be so—
> I do not love.
>
> Are known, but I—
> Will no one show
> I argued ill?
> Because, although
> Self-sentenced, still
> I keep my trust.

The verse continues for a few lines, to break off in the
middle of a parenthetical clause. Readers may think the
"self-sentenced" genius does argue ill; but he argues by
referring to Christ's words, "By their fruits ye shall
know them" (Matthew 7:16), comparing himself to

both the earthly fruit-bearing tree and the heavenly tree, the pattern set by Christ, which would bear fruit in love. He is too conscientious to believe he can approach Christ's pattern.

Men have such moods as seasons change. Winter brings death, and sometimes trees are barren. Again and again in Hopkins, earth's moods, seasons, and cycle of mortality are set off against the divine seasons, temporary spring against eternal Easter, and brief May against the endless season of Mary. In his very eary "Spring and Death" the poet already sees mortality in freshness:

> It seem'd an evening in the Spring:
> —a little sickness in the air
> From too much fragrance everywhere.

He describes the figure of Death among the flowers, marking them for their autumnal graves: "It seem'd so hard and dismal thing, / Death, to mark them in the Spring." [5] Only from the symbolic seasons, derived from the Christian paradox of the Eternal incarnate in time, is death exorcised. Although Christ's winelike blood, being a sacrament, was and is physical as well as

[5] Gardner comments on these undated lines: "This poem strongly suggests the influence of the father, Manley Hopkins, whose fanciful vein it resembles." See *Poems of Gerard Manley Hopkins* (4th ed.; London, 1967) p. 247. But there is little here of that rather heavy-handed playfulness the elder Hopkins displays in, for instance, an address from *Spicilegium Poeticum,* "To the Dodo:" "Queen Dido died! O Dodo, do you do / The deed she did, and die as dead as she!"

heavenly, while St. Dorothea's miraculous fruits, once exposed to the air, soon died, the timeless pattern that informs all time, the undated truth implicit in the Church calendar, can be thought of as resolving while stating the paradox of immortality in mortal forms and terms. The statement may be radically imperfect, but as priests and poets can use only the images of earthly experience, Hopkins can write of Christ's and the Virgin's perfect seasons only as echoed and imaged in the mortal seasons. If Gardner is right in ascribing the lines "Ad Mariam" to Hopkins, the poet has tried there, in Swinburne's accents, to transform the month, "Spring's one daughter," not into one of Swinburne's eternal earth goddesses but into the eternal season of Mary triumphant over death and winter.[6] In the lines "Rosa Mystica" this transformation is made perfectly clear:

'The Rose in a mystery'—where is it found?
Is it anything true? Does it grow upon ground?
It was made from earth's mould, but it went from man's
eyes
And its place is a secret, and shut in the skies.
    In the Gardens of God, in the daylight divine
    Find me a place by thee, Mother of mine.

Mary is rooted in history, in time, but her spot in the holy land is only where she once was. She and Christ are both, now, in *and* out of time:

[6] Bridges thought the poem so much like Swinburne that it could not be Hopkins. See Gardner's note in the fourth edition, p. 253.

What was its season, then? How long ago?
When was the summer that saw the bud blow?
Two thousands of years are near upon past
Since its birth, and its bloom, and its breathing its last.
  In the Gardens of God, in the daylight divine
  I shall keep time with thee, Mother of mine.

The phrase "keep time" has a special sense, not that of marking time by minute, hour, season, and year, but rather that of "holding" time, controlling and sustaining it—as, in "The Golden Echo," a care for all the beautiful things of time is "kept" only in Heaven. But this poem about Mary the rose-bush and Christ the miraculous rose she produced, about a season now beyond time, is more fanciful and less worked out than the mature and splendid "May Magnificat," which definitely and repeatedly plays upon a traditional source of paradox in the Christian lyric, the use of seasonal nature to express the supernatural beyond all brief seasons. There, the question of why May is the month of Mary can be answered by answering another question: "What is Spring?— / Growth in everything." Springtime, Maytime, is the month of birth for birds and trees and flowers, the month of "Nature's motherhood." And Mary is the ideal mother. But more than this, Spring is the time of joy, of "ecstasy all through mothering earth," that tells of Mary's joy in Christ's coming.

There are two sorts of nature poems possible for Hopkins, one of imperfect delight in the landscape, containing an awareness of its seasonal, ephemeral, term, and one of unmixed delight that is to be enjoyed only when landscape and season become sacramental by being both real and images of a higher reality. Then not only the fruits and flowers but also the bright times of year seem to be more than metaphorical and yet also more than literal, as the divine in nature is more than abstract and yet also more than earthly. Hopkins' only celebrations of seasonal "flesh and fleece, fur and feather," strawberries, blue eggs, "drop-of-blood-and-foam-dapple / Bloom," greybell, and cuckoo, which end in unmixed pleasure, are those that end by reference to the divine, as "The May Magnificat" does.

> This ecstasy all through mothering earth
> Tells Mary her mirth till Christ's birth
>   To remember and exultation
>   In God who was her salvation.

In part, no doubt, turning nature's times to the uses of religion is a preacher's technique. "The Silver Jubilee," for instance, celebrating the twenty-fifth year of an episcopate, as "Nature's round" makes an occasion, might be compared to Newman's imaginative passages at the beginning of his well-known sermon "The Second Spring." [7] Yet there is more than a conventional

[7] Hopkins' own sermons, however, are rather less likely to elaborate on natural, seasonal images—at least, as they are represented in Christopher Devlin's collection of *Sermons and Devotional Writings of Gerard Manley Hopkins* (London, 1959).

device in Hopkins' frequent references to season and seasonal vegetation. His deeply personal and always specific response to real things in nature is quite clear, and so, very often, is his response to days and dates. He responds to Christmas in a fragment in which he prays to be "freed" "From the self that I have been" and asks God with more hope than Tennyson could on the Christmases of *In Memoriam*, "Now begin, on Christmas day"; and he responds to Easter in the lines so titled:

> Gather gladness from the skies;
> Take a lesson from the ground;
> Flowers do ope their heavenward eyes
> And a Spring-time joy have found;
> Earth throws Winter's robes away,
> Decks herself for Easter Day.
>
> . . . . .
>
> Henceforth let your souls alway
> Make each morn an Easter Day.

The religious sentiment may be commonplace, but the language and imagery are more than derived, more than literary or homiletic. Even in such relatively undistinguished verse the poet communicates a distinct unwavering love for the things of time, for the divine really incarnate.

So, although dates and seasons can, like earthly creatures, be perceived as beautiful but imperfect languages all saying heavenly truths, they retain the substance, the intrinsic shape and worth, that Hopkins emphasizes in language itself, especially the language of poetry, delighting in its very sounds for their own sakes. And although some moments of sheer delight in the season are possible when the season is taken in its eternal meaning, as flowers and fruits in certain lights are temporal images or sacramentals of eternal flowering and fruitfulness, both times and things retain their hauntingly imperfect aspect. Hopkins has just enough of the mystic's desire for completion, for oneness with the perfect, to long repeatedly for these times to transcend time, fulfilling their shapes and worths. Even the Church, in his poem of 1879, is "Time's Andromeda" waiting for her deliverance by Perseus, Christ, who "lingers and leaves her to her extremes," "Her flower, her piece of being, doomed dragon's food." Ordinary men can never here redeem their times, can only dwindle, as the very evergreen does.

> No, the tropic tree
> Has not a charter that its sap shall last
> Into all seasons, though no Winter cast
> The happy leafing. It is so with me.[8]

In "The Bugler's First Communion," "The Handsome Heart," "Brothers," and the lines "On the Portrait of Two Beautiful Young People," youth and springtime beauty touch Hopkins with a sense both sweet and melancholy. For men as for nature he desires that youth

[8] From "The Beginning of the End," 1865 ("My love is lessened and must soon be past").

be held, beauty kept, that springtime not dwindle. The earthly "Heaven-Haven," subtitled "A nun takes the veil," dramatizes this attitude: "I have desired to go / Where Springs not fail" (*Springs* can be taken as both sources of water and seasons),

> And I have asked to be
> Where no storms come,
> Where the green swell is in the heavens dumb,
> And out of the swing of the sea.

If these lines suggest a rather simple and idealized view of the cloistered life, or of any possible human life, the view is later to be changed in those parts of "The Deutschland" that show nuns who do not escape at all from the stress of storms, "the swing of the sea."

The season of spring is often poignantly associated with man's youth, soon gone; and both nature's and man's springtimes are to be held onto only in Heaven. This is the burden of the poem entitled "Spring," with its ecstatic description of weeds, eggs, the song of the thrush, pear leaves and blooms, and racing lambs.

> What is all this juice and all this joy?
> A strain of the earth's sweet being in the beginning
> Eden garden—Have, get, before it cloy,
> Before it cloud, Christ, lord, and sour with sinning,
> Innocent mind and mayday in girl and boy,
> Most, O maid's child, thy choice and worthy the
> winning.

Again the landscape serves, in spring, to remind men of Eden, the pattern of nature, and also to point toward the source of Eden's glory and the end of man. But it is only a "strain" that does this; juice and joy will in time "cloud" and "sour," as youthful innocence will fade. Even in his most enthusiastic moments, as in "Hurrahing in Harvest," the poet knows all this, knows that he must look for the moment to get, to "glean" from nature the higher promise. To get and glean, to catch the full meaning of landscape, is to see Christ in it, and that requires not only a time and a scape but also receptive eyes:

> These things, these things were here and but the beholder
>   Wanting; which two when they once meet,
> The heart rears wings bold and bolder
>   And hurls for him, O half hurls earth for him off under
>   his feet.

This is to say that in brief moments when man sees beyond nature, he is half rapt beyond earth. Still, the moments are brief, and he is only "half" out of the natural, imperfect world.

For, as we observe once more, Hopkins' is a world of halves and doubles, of signs and of times unfulfilled. Men do not always respond to nature, and so the beholder is wanting—as in "The Valley of Elwy" apparently, the Welsh do not "correspond" to the beauty around them, to the landscape of Wales. (Echoing lines in "The Deutschland," the poem asks God, "mighty a master," "a father and fond," to balance the two, people and land.) Or they respond with only the awareness that landscape beauty is ephemeral, forgetting Eden the

source and spring of spring and forgetting the means
for saving youth and brightness. This is the means pre-
scribed in "Morning Midday and Evening Sacrifice," a
poem about what nature tells men—

> This, all this beauty blooming,
> This, all this freshness fuming,
> Give God while worth consuming—

and repeated in "The Golden Echo"—"Give beauty
back, beauty, beauty, beauty, back to God, beauty's
self and beauty's giver." If aware at all of nature, men
become aware for the most part of how youth and
spring give way to age and autumn. They hear "The
Leaden Echo," grey the echo of brightness; "age and
age's evils" the echo of youth's loveliness; death the
echo of life. The two echoes make up one reality for
Hopkins, as they make up one poem, filled with repeat-
ings, re-echoings. "Spare" echoes "despair," the first of
the second half echoes the last of the first half; but the
sound is so curtailed that it means something new, both
"spare yourself this melancholy" and "there is a spare, a
single, hope for life." All the re-echoings reinforce the
idea that what has seemed at first a value to be kept,
fresh natural beauty with its echoing overtone of mortality, is really itself only an echo of a yet earlier single
value, something Edenic and now lost to the pied or
dappled or echoing world. The "Golden Echo" of the
second part speaks of what is not an echo at all but the
original.

Still, and he returns to this point as a fact of life

which has therefore to be a fact of poetry, Hopkins believes that men hear only echoes of the original, tell half-truths, perceive realities that only partake of reality, because they live here and not "yonder." Paradoxically, the echoes, words, and realities still have to be cherished for themselves if they are to reveal at all what is there beyond. Hopkins' imagery is like the symbolism of Wordsworth and Coleridge in that it has to be immanent in order to be transcendent.

Hopkins uses the seasons and seasonal vegetation, then, in several ways. First, he can at moments delight in the landscape of spring and summer, although the delight is mixed, as in so much Victorian poetry—unless it leads to the contemplation of supernatural objects. Now and then he adopts the traditional iconography of fruits and flowers, of Christ as the bunch of grapes and of miraculous or heavenly fruitfulness. More often, he uses the seasons in the familiar Christian way, celebrating Christmas and Easter not only as times of year but also as timeless times, as moments in history that are recurrently marked by the church calendar, yet point out of history to an eternal dispensation. Finally, and most often, he combines a deep concern for seasons and the things of time with a deep concern for eternal verity by contrasting, either explicitly or implicitly, the intensely delightful world of youth and spring, which however implies age and wintry death, with a perfected world of ageless youth and endless spring.

The literal landscape, overtones of traditional iconography, some of the religious meaning of the seasons, and certainly the sense of both life and death in the seasonal life, which must look to a life beyond, are all included in his short and apparently simple poem "Spring and Fall." The poem actually has rich overtones and itself implies echoes. It is, for all its brevity and seeming simplicity—and in part because of these qualities—one of Hopkins' finest achievements.

Subtitled, and addressed, "To a young child," the poem may be compared to similar addresses, such as Wordsworth's admonition to the "seer blest," the prophetic child of his Immortality ode; and with Arnold's sad lines "To a Gipsy Child by the Sea-Shore." There is no doubt that Hopkins' mood is very much closer to that of his Victorian contemporary who has described the gipsy child's poignant "majesty of grief." If, like Wordsworth and unlike Arnold, he relates his child very closely to the landscape and indeed concerns himself with the child's giving meaning to and taking meaning from the scene, that meaning seems to be wholly one of mourning for death in nature.[9] The Romantic, Wordsworthian, child, the visionary, has become the

---

[9] For Wordsworth's child, to be sure, the transaction is not conscious, as it is for the poet:

> The clouds that gather round the setting sun
> Do take a sober colouring from an eye
> That hath kept watch o'er man's mortality;
>
> . . . . .
>
> To me the meanest flower that blows can give
> Thoughts that do often lie too deep for tears.

Victorian child, more victim than visionary. But she is
also more than "the child." She is a specific person, is
given a name. As usual, Hopkins's interest is in the
individual.

The speaker begins by asking her two questions.

> Margaret, are you grieving
> Over goldengrove unleaving?
> Leaves, like the things of man, you
> With your fresh thoughts care for, can you?

"Goldengrove" is the mass of trees in glorious autumn
foliage. Ironically, their being golden, apparently precious, beautiful, and long-lasting, even timeless, is in
natural fact a sign of their being ephemeral, withered,
soon to die. The double sense of the term, however, is
less striking than the ambiguity of the modifier "unleav-
ing," which could mean "not leaving," "remaining"—as
the golden grove could be related to the golden echo
and be an unchanging heavenly grove, or even Eden—
but in an ordinary time and place could mean only
"losing its leaves"; the parallel word is "undressing."
The child grieves "over" yellow leaves quite literally, as
they lie of the ground. The next question is both rhetorical and involuted in its syntax, "Can you, with your
fresh thoughts, care for leaves, as you can for the things
of man?" And the implied answer is affirmative. It is not
quite that the shades of Wordsworth's prison house are
falling on the child, or that the viewer "gives" to nature
a knowledge of mortality, but rather that the young

fresh mind takes from seasonal nature, as it must if it cares at all for leaves, trees, and all the bright objects in the landscape, a sad understanding of how time works. The images of nature are images of death, the fresh mind knows, for it is fresh not only in being young but also in coming fresh to phenomena and seeing them as they are. It is as if Hopkins were replying to Words-worth and saying that dulling custom does not intro-duce the idea of death but blurs and overlooks it—that children are more freshly touched, even wounded, by grief, by loss, by the simple fact of mortality, than adults are.

> Ah, as the heart grows older
> It will come to such sights colder
> By and by, nor spare a sigh
> Though worlds of wanwood leafmeal lie;
> And yet you *will* weep and know why.

At least the poet can agree with both Wordsworth and Arnold that the young child has a more immediate perception of things than the adult. The heart has not yet grown cold. But where Wordsworth takes this per-ception to be one of life and joy, and Arnold takes it to be a profound and virtually tragic perception of the poignant reality of life—a "majesty of grief"—Hopkins finds it to be a direct, mournful, and for the time unmit-igated vision of hard mortal reality, not deeply poetic or tragic but terribly melancholy. With every autumn, "worlds of wanwood" fall, the groves of all nature turn wan, pale, or yellow, and their leaves lie piecemeal in their annual deaths. Yet only the child, who sees the dying of fall for the first time, and perhaps the poet who has to see it again and again if he is still to see clearly the brilliance of spring and summer, can face the present truth. There is an adversative in the ninth line, "And yet you will weep and know why." This is the first extra line in the rhyme scheme, as lines seven, eight, and nine make up the only triplet in a poem of couplets, a poem about the duality of spring and fall. Here, the third point is that the adult who is blinded by custom to death all around him is nevertheless forced to sigh and even to weep for specific losses, knowing why he does so in that he locates the source of grief as the death of a particular thing or person. He feels a special pain even if he ignores the general truth.

The general truth, yoking man and nature for the time being, is what this poem is leading to: the limited but valid truth that the death which a child finds in an autumn scene is what she will find in herself. She may not name it death, but

> Now no matter, child, the name:
> Sorrow's springs are the same.

In this couplet one of the two key words of the title occurs, and it has several meanings. "Sorrow's springs" are both the early, springtime appearances of sorrow and the sources of sorrow. Not only has all childhood grief a common nature; the sources of all human sadness are ultimately one source, one fact. And the one fact is the other key word in the title of this poem, the fall. The word "blight" occurs later, but the "fall" of its title is not repeated within the poem. The season fall is evidently implied by the yellow falling leaves, and the larger sense of the word, the Fall of man, is implied by the large subject of mortality, for the poem is about fallen nature, the falls of life that result from man's original sin. "Spring" means a season, youth, and a source. "Fall" means a season, age, and a downfall or dying. While in these series of meanings the first two are opposed—spring in contrast with fall, youth in contrast with age—the third meanings, the senses of source and of downfall, draw together. In these lines addressed to a girl in her youth, her springtime, who is seeing nature in its age, its season of fall, the spring or source of sorrow is, by implication, just the Fall of man from which all falls have sprung. This is for Hopkins the origin of natural and human mortality, and the meaning, therefore, of the saying, "Sorrow's springs are the same": its ultimate spring is man's Fall.

Not that explication, punning, or theology can ever fully clarify the mystery of spring and fall.

> Nor mouth had, no nor ever mind expressed
> What heart heard of, ghost guessed:
> It is the blight man was born for,
> It is Margaret you mourn for.

The poet's words, the philosopher's thought, are not adequate to express what the feelings tell and what the spirit, whether prompted or not by the Holy Ghost, knows instinctively. The sense of radical imperfection, apparently, is inborn, a flaw even of the inscape, and so the blight is part of every self in nature.

If this poem about the self in nature reveals how different Hopkins can be from Wordsworth in the Immortality ode and even from Arnold in his address to a gipsy child, the contrasts themselves suggest clearly, once again, the great extent to which he shares their Romantic and post-Romantic interests. "Spring and Fall" is not only about seasonal time; it is also specifically about childhood. Like so many writers of his century, Hopkins sees man's situation by observing and sharing the undimmed perception of the very young. To him the "young child" is a significant figure.

For Romantic writers the child is likely to signify man in his original and essential being, without guile or artifice. The first of the great English Romantics, Blake, shows us childhood as a time of innocence, but of innocence necessarily short-lived. Experience inevitably comes, experience of a world in which the child is used and abused by men. The Romantic child, then, the human being pure and simple, can be a sufferer as well as a seer: the very simplicity that allows him to see a divine beauty to which older, corrupted eyes and minds are blinded makes him liable to abuse. Wordsworth may be inclined to describe children as seers only, but Coleridge's innocent Christabel is clearly designed to suffer, and even Byron's young Juan, hardly a Word-

sworthian prophet, represents a perceptive and spontaneous nature victimized by society. If, however, the
Romantic child can be both a visionary and a victim,
the poignancy of the second term derives from the
power of the first. It is painful to realize that those
creatures who see and feel most truly are those least
heeded, most harmed. The verse of Hood may provide
an exception, but the sufferings of Romantic children
and child-like people are generally moving because of
their sheer virtue more than their pitiful vulnerability.

With the Victorians, once more, there is a shift in
emphasis. The child in Victorian literature is much
more likely to be a victim than to be a visionary. Or,
rather, if both terms can be used, the importance of the
first derives from that of the second. The child can see
clearly, but what he sees now is that he himself *is* a
victim of human nature and of time. Dickens may
sometimes idealize his children so that they seem virtually prophetic in their simple wisdom and angelic in
their purity; but more than anything else, they are
deeply pathetic because they are cruelly forced to understand their own weakness.[10] The terrible truth that

[10] Still, Dickens of all the Victorians most nearly balances
and combines the two roles for the child, that of moral norm
and that of pathetic victim; Sissy in *Hard Times,* for example,
is the moral center of the novel, and the other characters are
finally to be judged according to the way they respond to
her spontaneous warmth. George Eliot's Eppie in *Silas Marner*
has a somewhat similar role but functions in perhaps a more
limited way.

Dickens reminds us of, with his children and child-like men made victims by a blind and heartless society, is that we are all like children in being weak, in being subject to other forces and other persons. Tennyson, who often turns theme into metaphor, defines himself as a child crying for the light—and, far from being a visionary child, he is unable to see or understand any great redeeming light. He is afraid he may be at the mercy of a nature that is alien and merciless.

The suffering of the Romantic child, then, is significant, as a reflection upon society, because he is an innocent visionary, responding truly to nature. The vision of the Victorian child is significant, as an insight into the human situation, because he sees with fresh and awful clarity that he himself, man himself, is a victim. Like Dickens and Meredith, Arnold and Tennyson, Hopkins recognizes the pathos of man's situation in the feelings of the child.

But he retains, along with this Victorian recognition, a faith that is different from and yet related to the Romantic faith in some immanent divinity. His Margaret may be fallen and mortal, but for Hopkins the child has also a divine source and an immortal soul. If men are victims and know it, a higher vision is still possible; and this is so because of the Timeless entering into time. The poet's ultimate subject is not temporal nature or the suffering self but the Incarnation set against these facts. And the imagery he uses to express this subject is one not of seasonal vegetation or animal form but of fiery light.

5 "That Nature Is a Heraclitean Fire"

Images of light, of fiery sunlight, starlight, moonlight, are everywhere in Hopkins, contrasted with and complemented by the images of shadow and of night. The poet's love for painting, his early desire to emulate the Pre-Raphaelites in art, and Ruskin's influence on him may have something to do with his interest in precise description of light effects and visual phenomena.[1] In fact, Hopkins can sometimes evoke a

[1] In his letters Hopkins comments frequently on painting as well as poetic and musical matters (see especially *The Letters of Gerard Manley Hopkins to Robert Bridges*, ed. Claude Colleer Abbott [revised edition; London, 1955]); but the clearest evidences of his interest are his essays on art and aesthetics and his notes and drawings—close observations of clouds, trees, and flowers—in *The Journals and Papers of Gerard Manley Hopkins* ed. Humphry House and Graham Storey (London, 1959). The drawings of dandelion, hemlock, ivy, of hedgerow leaves and branches, and of rock in a cliff copse, showing a Ruskin-like concern for accurate detail, resemble in style the work not only of Ford Madox Brown but also of Ruskin himself.

brightly lit and shaded landscape more vividly than the painter-poet Dante Rossetti does.

Of course, his concern for just how things are lit and how they look is by no means unique in his times; the criterion of exact fidelity to nature, applied to painter and poet alike, is generally accepted in Victorian criticism of the arts, and it is not only Ruskin who describes in words or represents in drawings how light and shadow define the forms of objects. It is a matter of visual accuracy, something that Tennyson, too, very much cares about.

While the imagery of light is literal for Hopkins and the poets of his century, it is also something more for them: for Wordsworth, the essence of nature is revealed in a glorious light seen clearly only by the young and innocent; and for Tennyson, Arnold, and Swinburne, daylight, nature's light, may be literally but also metaphorically both creative and destructive. The special quality of Hopkins' poems about light is their way of distinguishing a devotion beautifully illuminated, to nature, which is to be represented faithfully, from a sense of nature's being fallen and alien, its light partly darkness. These two attitudes toward nature, toward the world of sunlight and stars, might be said to alternate in other Victorian poets; in Hopkins they occur simultaneously. We have observed that one of his favorite adjectives is *dappled;* his world is double in a pictorial sense and in a metaphorical one, always being dappled with sun and shadow. In ocean, in landscape, and in all creatures he finds harsh, fleeting beauty and imperfectly reflected, echoed power and grace.

Sometimes Hopkins' symbolic doubleness is implicit, however. For him the poet's eye must be like the painter's eye. It is an eye for detail, for precisely how the light defines or the shadow obscures. Now and then, in fact, he attempts no more in his verse (especially the early verse) than to describe detail, to catch bright glints of light with hardly a suggestion of the symbolic—as in his lovely and almost impressionistic lines entitled "Moonrise." In that exercise, written in 1876,

The moon dwindled and thinned to the fringe of a finger-
  nail held to the candle,
Or paring of paridisäical fruit, lovely in waning but
  lustreless,

is seen as

      the prized, the desirable sight, unsought, presented
    so easily, [that]
Parted me leaf and leaf, divided me, eyelid and eyelid of
  slumber.[2]

But it is much more characteristic of him to move from such vivid and excited description to a comment on how the lights of nature are created and kept by divine forces.

[2] The upper and lower lids are like leaves opened as the sleeper is awakened by the moonlight.

Hopkins' sonnet "God's Grandeur" begins and ends in the imagery of brightness:

> The world is charged with the grandeur of God.
> It will flame out, like shining from shook foil.

The word "charged," as the rest of the octave might indicate, can mean both that physical nature is sustained by a powerful force, such as a charge of electricity, and that this world, including man, has divinely created beauty in its charge, in its keeping. The principle of instress here makes brilliant inscape flash forth. Physical beauty can best be shown when things like gold foil and shining oil are shaken and crushed. (The parallel with the ending of "The Windhover" seems evident.) But men have no right to ignore or tread down natural beauty; and when they blear and smudge it, they are failing their charge, failing to heed or "reck" God's power, his "rod." The following lines echo both Ruskin's attacks on the commercializing and polluting of landscape and Wordsworth's plaint, "The world is too much with us; . . . / Getting and spending, we lay waste our powers, / Little we see in nature that is ours":

> And all is seared with trade; bleared, smeared with toil;
> And wears man's smudge and shares man's smell: the soil
> Is bare now, nor can foot feel, being shod.

This last line of the octave suggests both barrenness in nature, nakedness or fruitlessness where there should be growing life, and, paradoxically, an artificial covering where there should be nakedness, for men ought to be able to feel nature directly with their skins and senses bared. (One imagines Hopkins' enjoyment in going barefoot.) But the major imagery of the poem is that of brightness, though it be bleared and smudged. So the sestet begins:

> And for all this, nature is never spent;
>> There lives the dearest freshness deep down things;
> And though the last lights off the black West went
>> Oh, morning, at the brown brink eastward, springs.

If man fails his charge, still the physical world retains, and adheres to, its charge: in the dappled order of spring and fall, of eastering dawn and westering darkness, light and life remain and return,

> Because the Holy Ghost over the bent
>> World broods with warm breast and with ah! bright
>>> wings.

The world is bent, perhaps, in that it is round, its horizon a curve.[3] But it is also a bent or partly crooked world, twisted out of the original mode of Eden, and so it needs to be sustained by constant grace. Since this is a poem about the light of nature, it is concerned more definitely with the creating power and authority of God the Father and the sustaining grace of the Holy Ghost, by whose bright wings light and warmth are

[3] Like other mid-Victorian artists, Hopkins is fond of drawing within circular forms, and a good many of his pictures, including "Vision of the Mermaids," are framed by a circle.

nurtured, than with the saving action and passion of Christ, from whose light men, especially—so Hopkins elsewhere declares—are to take their lights. The principle of Christian instress is only hinted at by the participles *shook* and *crushed*, and the one duty of men touched upon is the duty not of Christian self-sacrifice but of recognizing and giving reverence to natural and sacramental objects.

One extraordinary fact about this poem on things is that so few things are clearly described in it. The shaken metal foil and heavy oil may be striking images, but the bare earth, shod foot, sunset and dawn seem not to be very definite. The very light imagery of the poem is effective but somewhat generalized, a bright but hazy glow.

In "The Starlight Night," however, light images are clear as well as brilliant. The stars are fancifully conceived of as "fire folk" sitting in their boroughs and citadels of the sky; they are like diamonds in the dark, like bright elves' eyes, "quickgold" sparkling on grey lawns, beams of white beaten small and brilliant by the wind, or snowflake-white doves—and the series of metaphors is as dazzling as it is gay in its extravagance; for, once more, the sense of how all things resemble each other, rhyming and chiming, is as exciting to Hopkins as the sense of how each thing is different, unique, "disseveral" in itself. Through all comparisons, however, and throughout the octave of this sonnet, the bright lights remain actual stars at which we are looking. The poem makes two statements about the stars. The first is like the admonition of "The Golden Echo": keep beauty by giving it back to God; that is, look to achieve the beauty of nature in a higher heavenly form by seeking the very source of nature. "Buy then! bid then!" with "Prayer, patience, alms, vows." The second is an assertion that the incarnate God is not only behind but also housed in and expressed by the starlight of nature, which is shut off from our eyes and partly revealed to us by the natural order, just as something housed can be suggested by the style of its building. The stars are finally, then, like a barn of paling of light that "shuts" in and yet tells of the bridegroom Chirst, His virgin mother, and all the saints.

Although Hopkins treats an apparently less concrete subject in "The Lantern Out of Doors," which is about "beauty bright / In mould or mind," here, too, it is first of all the light of nature that he cares about. And nature, to Hopkins, never means anything so abstract as Carlyle's invisible force or Mill's sum of principles that govern all things and their actions. It means palpable bodies and other inscaped objects, as well as the landscapes they occupy. "The Lantern Out of Doors," beginning with the experience of an actual image, goes no further toward abstraction than to find in this a figure of speech for the real, not abstract, physical beauty of body, movement, and voice. The lit lantern can easily become the sign and the extension of a person, as the lantern of Diogenes does; this lantern, in fact, represents a person who lights up the darkness. But one may see only the lantern and wonder who carries it, as one may see the face and figure or hear the voice of a person, have some momentary impression of his unique reality, his inscape, and still wonder what lies behind the impression of beauty or brightness. Through God's grace and their own consequent gracefulness, men do communicate their unique selves to each other, but they do so imperfectly and ephemerally in an imperfect, emphemeral, bent world. With their rare beauties they brighten the dull air—"rain against" it with rays of light—only "till death or distance buys them quite." And, the speaker now declares, however I turn and strain (or "wind") my eyes after the bright figure that moves into the distance of time (toward death) or space (toward disappearance), "I cannot" see it finally, "and out of sight is out of mind." For, again, the poet's mind dwells on the visible and tangible. The proverb, startlingly familiar in the midst of Hopkins' original phrasing, is not at all a lapse in diction, but it is used as a familiar and dull truth, a truism, with which to contrast a sharp, bright, better truth. Out of eyesight is *not* out of Christ's mind; for Christ's grace, which makes limited, temporary communication possible between men, consists in an unlimited, lasting comprehension of each man. This comprehension is identical with caring, so that to "mind" is, for Him, both to have full cognizance and to be deeply concerned about men.

Christ minds; Christ's interest, what to avow or amend
  There, eyes them, heart wants, care haunts, foot follows
                             kind,
Their ransom, their rescue, and first, fast, last friend.

Christ is neither uninterested, nor disinterested—for all
men are like him, and his proper concern in what is his
and in his image is an interest in what qualities of an
individual man he can accept, or wed to himself, and in
what he must mend. This interest keeps his eye on those
who are out of all other eyesight. His heart desires,
attention presses upon, and—as in Francis Thompson's
"Hound of Heaven"—his foot pursues his own kind or
kindred, and does so kindly. Whereas "God's Grandeur" begins with the lights of landscape nature and
ends with the Holy Ghost who keeps the world warm,
and whereas "The Starlight Night" begins with sky-
scape imagery and ends with the inhabitants of Heaven
—Christ and all the saints as well—of whom that imagery may remind us, "The Lantern Out of Doors"
begins with a light man holds and carries and ends with
the single figure of Christ, the archetype of man's peculiar and especially inscaped bodily self. Yet each of
these three brilliant sonnets makes the images of light
express earthly nature, the nature of land, sky, and
men's physical forms, which in itself implies and looks
to Heaven.

    There is another, related, way in which Hopkins uses
such imagery to express the inner, moral, or spiritual

qualities of men. To be sure, "The Lantern Out of Doors" involves "mind" as well as "mould"; but its being out of doors emphasizes the external and visible aspect of the natural man. Its companion sonnet, "The Candle Indoors," stresses instead the other inseparable aspect of human selfhood, the interior quality that mould or manner may hint at, as the expression on a person's face may tell his mood, but cannot entirely reveal. Hopkins may sometimes casually refer to men's spirits as fires, inner lights, and candles. In "Margaret Clitheroe," for instance, the saint's fawning false friends try "with tears to put her candle out." "The Candle Indoors," however, develops the image, beginning once again not with the metaphor but with the actual experience that suggests it. In the first person, it relates how one yellow light can "put back" night's darkness. The beams of light, responding to (they "truckle at") the movement of eyelashes, seem to play brightly to and fro. (The precise artist's observation of this effect reminds us how important to Hopkins *looking* is, the active relationship between the unique object and the uniquely seeing viewer.) Not knowing who works by the candle, the poet is all the more eager that whoever it is, she or he, "Jessy or Jack," may be there with some good purpose, at some task to glorify God. Then he expostulates with himself to come "indoors, come home" out of the darkness and attend to, trim and keep bright, his own "vital candle," his "fading fire," in the tight inner vault of his heart.

You there are master, do your own desire;
What hinders? Are you beam-blind, yet to a fault
In a neighbor deft-handed? Are you that liar
And, cast by conscience out, spendsavor salt?

Like the word "there" in the eighth line of the poem, which is made emphatic by the pause after it, the "there" in the eleventh line is to be stressed. A man is master in one place, in his own heart or inner life, and there, as nowhere else, he has the free will to do exactly his own desire. His desire should be to keep a light burning that, however he works by it, glorifies God. The sonnet ends not with a direct reference to the Deity, to the Holy Ghost or Christ, but rather with lessons given in Christ's own parabolic words. First, punning on the words, Hopkins alludes to the story (from Matthew 7:4–5 and Luke 6:42) of the fault-finding hypocrite, "that liar," who can quickly (or is "deft-handed" to) see the mote in his neighbor's eye and yet is unaware of the beam in his own. "Beam" here means both a large object and a beam of light, so that to be "beam-blind" is to be blinded to the light and at the same time to have one's own beam of light, or spiritual life, blotted out by any such obstacle. Then Hopkins refers to Christ's metaphor of salt, which occurs three times in the gospels: "Ye are the salt of the earth: but if the salt have lost his savour . . . it is thenceforth good for nothing." Finally, we may think of yet another parable. The earlier purely visual interest in both the light seen and the way of seeing it has its counterpart in

the poet's concern for both the fact of the spiritual
flame and its being seen by others, its brightening the
dark world, in both the fact of salty savor and its
function of preserving and wholesomely flavoring
other substance. The biblical passage of which Hopkins
is evidently reminded by the sight of a candle is that
which comes immediately after the "salt of the earth"
passage in the Gospel of Matthew (5:13–16) and is
followed by the parable of the beam:

Ye are the light of the world. A city that is set on an hill
cannot be hid.
Neither do men light a candle, and put it under a bushel,
but on a candlestick; and it giveth light unto all that are
in the house.
Let your light so shine before men, that they may see your
good works, and glorify your Father which is in Heaven.

The light that is to shine is precisely the Christlike
self. And the same imagery of illuminating fire is used
to explain this in the lines beginning, "As kingfishers
catch fire, dragonflies draw flame." Like "The Windhover," this poem ascends from the animal figure to
the human, seeing a human meaning in the lower creatures. But the poem is not so much about instress, about
the buckling of proud self, as about inscape, the very
essential quality of self which is, to begin with, an inner
spiritual quality that mortal eyes glimpse only in moments when personal style or spirit flashes forth. For
there are moments of great grace given in beauty as

well as moments of grace given in stress that demands self-sacrifice. Another sonnet, the "kingfisher" poem, devotes an octave to both animal and inanimate inscapes and a sestet to the higher scape of man. It moves, that is, from forms in which style and physical appearance are one to a form in which they are double, for man has an outer as well as an inner style; he has a personality that in part expresses and yet is in part external to the spiritual self. In both lower and higher forms, inscape or the principle of the special self is still to be understood as something intrinsic that communicates, "tells," "speaks," or cries itself. Almost all of the dozen verbs in the octave are significantly active, even vigorous, and some of them are doubly significant. To "catch fire" is to be set on fire as the kingfisher appears to be when it flashes in the light, but it is also to grasp fire—as when the poet declares he "caught" the windhover this morning—and so it means not only to reflect passively but to *act* as a reflector. To "draw flame" is to draw light to oneself, but for the draftsman Hopkins it could also mean to delineate a fire, artfully, and in one's own style to represent (or re-present) light. The other verbs and images do not suggest light flashing forth, but they all describe the action of the self making itself known: each pebble falling into the rim of the round well-rings in its own way, each bell swinging in an arc or bow peals out its special sound to "tell" its own name; and these examples are summed up in the line "Each mortal thing does one thing and the same." The repeated first word of the poem, "As," is both logical and temporal, meaning that just as all these things speak in their own styles, so every object is acting *when* all these sights are seen and sounds are heard. "Like" in the third line seems to be used for "as," connecting the verbs "tells" and "finds"; and even though it offends the English teacher's ear, it may have the purpose of pointing toward a paradoxical likeness of all things to each other that is summed up in the fifth line about "each" "one." The likeness is paradoxical because each creature is like every other in acting absolutely as itself, showing itself unique and thus unlike any other. After the colon the last lines of the octave explain that everything

> Deals out that being indoors each one dwells;
> Selves—goes itself; *myself* it speaks and spells;
> Crying *What I do is me: for that I came.*

The being that dwells indoors each one is the candle indoors, the light of self. And all the preceding verbs are contained in the coined verb "selves," meaning "declares itself by being itself"—for, again, inscape both *is* and *acts* or communicates itself. Everything "goes itself" in the sense that dogs "go" bow-wow, cats "go" meow, and so on. So this octave that begins with light ends with sound, with speech, proceeding from imagery to declaration, from visual to verbal. And the last phrase, "I came," is one of movement that may easily have oblique reference to Christ's first coming, for the selves of all creatures, windhover, kingfisher, and dragonfly, are like Christ only in a lower and lesser sense than men are.

Man himself is the subject of the sestet. Now the poet says more than in the octave because now his subject is more complex. A man is not only a unique being but also a complicated and doubly special one, so that for him to "selve," to be and express himself fully, is to sustain an intensely indoors, spiritual, life, as well as an outer style, appearance, and speech.[4] The "just man" is himself when he "justices," both acts justly and is within himself just; and a just man is not only the man whose acts are fair, he is the person who *is* truly, justly, man: he is the whole, the real, man. He "keeps grace," and that keeping "keeps all his goings graces": his life remains humanly graceful, beautiful in its external actions, insofar as he retains the divine grace that created him. So he

> Acts in God's eye what in God's eye he is—
> Christ—for Christ plays in ten thousand places,
> Lovely in limbs, and lovely in eyes not his
> To the Father through the features of men's faces.

Christ "plays" in men's features as light plays on shiny surfaces, because men reflect, "catch," or "draw" fire even more brilliantly than other creatures. And the fire

---

[4] Christopher Devlin's comment on inscape, as Hopkins uses that term in his essay "On Personality, Grace and Free Will," is apt: apparently inscape, for Hopkins, is essentially natural, and man's truest shape, or soul, is something of a higher order. See *The Sermons and Devotional Writings . . .* , p. 146.

they reflect and also participate in, as they embody it, make it freshly incarnate, is that of Christ. The more a man is just, or truly himself, the more closely he resembles and in fact the more nearly he *is* Christ—although the mode by which each man moves toward, never reaching, that perfect uniqueness of light, is a unique mode.[5] Each just man is in some degree Christ, and yet his own bodily features are "not his," not Christ's. Again the paradox is that of identity and difference, or of human diversity and divine unity. This paradox communicated by the final visual imagery, the light imagery of Christ playing in men's forms so that God can see Himself there, is based on the paradox of the Incarnation, of God both in human mortal form and, at the same time, immortal and perfect.

The lines that ask, "To what serves mortal beauty?" are about not all mortal things but only human beings —about the bodily beauty of men, and, at last, about men's innermost beauty, their immortal grace. But first and most of all, the poem is concerned with the visible loveliness of human bodies. This may be "dangerous" in several ways. It sets the blood of the beholder "dancing," and these words hint at the danger of lust (even though Hopkins rarely dwells on active sin and least of

[5] The paradox is partly theological—as in Duns Scotus—but it is related, too, to Ruskin's teaching about an artist's true style appearing when he tries most earnestly to represent what he sees (without trying to have a style). Similarly, Hopkins might say that a man most fully expresses himself in the imitation of Christ.

all on sinful sexual appetites). It can also lead to pride, as men's features and self-flinging movements can be "prouder" than music; pride, after all, may mean either a legitimately noble style or the first of sins.[6] Yet, all of this negative qualification is rather parenthetical, for the poem is a defense of human beauty and a definition of its function. It serves men, and it can serve God. We are told to "see," which means once more, as the imperative "look" does in "The Starlight Night," that we are to perceive through vision as well as to understand beauty intellectually. Then we shall know how it

keeps warm

Men's wits to the things that are; what good means—where

a glance

Master more may than a gaze, gaze out of countenance.

A momentary revelation of personal gracefulness, such as the Windhover's buckling or the kingfisher's sudden flash, often yields more truth than staring, interrogation, or analysis can elicit. The familiar story of Pope Gregory's seeing the blond captive Britons, declaring, "Non Angli sed Angeli," and sending missionaries to their land, is clear and relevant enough. But its implication, too, has to be worked out. Hopkins perhaps imagines that Gregory was as sensitive to the personal beauty of men as he himself is; and what he himself knows to be most dangerous about the response to such

[6] Again, as in the poem dedicated to him, the composer Purcell is given as the pattern of inscape, of personal style, in art.

beauty is the desire, not necessarily or only sensual, to hold, fix, and possess physical beauty for its own sake. This desire for something impossible violates the law of religion.

Our law says: Love what are love's worthiest, were all
known;
World's loveliest—men's selves. Self flashes off frame and
face.

Self, soul, or full inscape is not identical with body and countenance, but it is expressed in part by these: if it "flashes off," the flash is brief and soon dies away, as frame and face decay.

What do then? how meet beauty? Merely meet it; own,
Home at heart, heaven's sweet gift; then leave, let that
alone.

To meet is not to hold; to own—that is, to avow or accept—the gift of beauty is not at all to own in the sense of possessing it. Bodily beauty, which is temporary and cannot be held onto, functions to show inner beauty and to remind men of beauty's source. When the poet finally advises, "Yea, wish that though, wish all, God's greater beauty, grace," "that" is the beautiful person who is to be left alone and wished the very best—not only outer gracefulness, the sign of a grace, but the actual inner grace that can exist with hardly a flash or sign. Like other poems about the lights, the beauties, of nature, this one concludes by referring to the higher light. But it does not at all deny the intensity of the lower and lesser. In fact, because human beauty is the most brilliant and exciting in all of nature, that to which the poet responds most fully, these poignant lines on beauty, love, and the necessity, for love of God and man, of leaving beauty alone are among the most moving Hopkins has written.

Still one danger of beauty is that it may nourish false pride, and this is the danger inherent in any human gracefulness or accomplishment. The fact that man's light is in the eye of heaven a little, precious thing, a "fire and fever fussy," is seen and perhaps exaggerated in the fascinating poem that begins,

> The shepherd's brow, fronting forked lightning, owns
> The horror and the havoc and the glory
> Of it.

Ironically, once more, to own is not to possess: the shepherd acknowledges the magnificence of external nature, but he himself lacks such magnificence. Men, awed by the story of the fallen angels (the poet has Milton in mind), know that they themselves are but "scaffold of brittle bones," short-lived, and pitiful, not grand: "What bass is *our* viol for tragic tones?" The consistent light imagery of this sonnet makes a contrast with the imagery of those poems that praise both the outer and the inner brilliance of man above all other lights in landscape nature. The imagery also prepares for but does not reach the final stage of the lines on nature as a "Heraclitean Fire." Man is, in the mood of this passage, a mere "Man Jack" whose physical state is more pitiful than appealing. Here, man is not the beautiful other I see but the dreary self I feel.

And I that die these deaths, that feed this flame,
That . . . in smooth spoons spy life's masque mirrowed:
                                                          tame
My tempests there, my fire and fever fussy.

Hopkins predicts now the way in which Victorian self-consciousness can finally become, as in Eliot's "Prufrock," a kind of self-mockery, with the inversion of all grand Romantic expectations. But the need for grandeur, the need to relate oneself to forked lightning, cosmic tragedy, the angels, is betrayed by his almost desperate tone. If man only feeds a Heraclitean flame with his little fire, if he cannot for the moment look beyond his mortal pettiness, then his mirror of life is no more than a spoon, his stormy emotions are tempests in a teacup, and his light is so dim as to be like a darkness.

Hopkins uses darkness to describe the dreary and sometimes dreadful sense of being only oneself, cut off from the glory of heaven:

I wake and feel the fell of dark, not day.
What hours, O what black hours we have spent
This night!

So begin the most terrible of all his lines on being oneself. In "Carrion Comfort," too, during inner tempest and suffering, the most the speaker can do is "wish day come" after the night "Of now done darkness [when] I wretch lay wrestling with (my God!) my God."

Yet, although man mourns his mortal self in darkness, as Margaret does in "Spring and Fall," the darkness is ambiguous and intermittent. Light and darkness inter- twined make up the major imagery of "Spelt from Sibyl's Leaves," which is about the mixed nature of this mortal world. Heavy baroque lines describe the strain- ing toward death of "hearse-of-all-night," but also the stars in "fire-featuring heaven." These lines concern the tendency of selves, of forms, to dissolve and be forgot- ten or dismembered—but also the oracular promise of something else. The dapple and the doubleness of earthly life seem to rush toward the singleness of night, of death; yet there remain two spools, two folds, two aspects of each reality, including self: light, white, right, as well as darkness, black, wrong. So "Self- wrung, selfstrung, sheathe- and shelterless, thoughts against thoughts in groans grind."

But behind the dappled world and its temporary darkness, and, at least in one sense, within the very darkness, Hopkins believes there is light. That is just the point that has been made by the language and im- agery of "The Deutschland." In that poem there are three versions of light: the lovely light of nature repre- sented by stars and the clear bright sky, sustained by the Holy Ghost; the fiery light of divine power repre- sented by lightning and "fire of stress," or flames of grace, the working of God the Father; and the light of virtue or grace incarnate represented perfectly in Christ, the kindly "heart's light," but also reflected in Christ-like man seen as a "beacon of light." It is necessary to pass from the first stage through the instress demanded by the second before reaching the third stage, which allows a full recognition of human—and Christ-imitating—inscape. And this means discovering that, just as in thunder there is lightning, so above and acting through the fact of mortal darkness there is still the light of divine power: "Thou art above, thou Orion of light." Christ is re-born through darkness and drowning.

Because Hopkins is a poet of doubleness, a poet of Christian paradox, he is misread when these three stages are separated from each other, or when he is taken not to have a single and consistent imaginative scheme. There are urgent tensions within his art, and indeed there is at the center of it a seeming contradiction, because there is a seeming contradiction at the center of Christian thought. But the several elements are almost always present, at least implicitly, in his verse. Hopkins does not express the conflict between, and alternating of, priest and artist, or devotional writer and nature poet, or ascetic and aesthete; and he does not sometimes believe that the landscape in which men live is wholly dark, nor does he sometimes believe that it is wholly bright. For him the world is dappled, even when he celebrates what he sees as the brightest moment in its history, the Incarnation of Christ.[7] "The Blessed Virgin Compared to the Air We Breathe" is like the passage on Christ's brilliant coming, stanza 34, in "The Deutschland" in that it represents Christ as a divine fire becoming a "kind" light, warm but not fiery and destructive. But man's dark element is not wholly forgotten.

In making his comparison, the poet probably has in mind not only the literal truth that earth's atmosphere filters the sun's harsh rays but also the iconography of the conception of Christ according to which the Virgin is shown with a single fiery ray from heaven—often, in paintings, coming through a window—to her womb. Yet, and characteristically, Hopkins begins with actual experience. The "needful" element of "world-mothering air" is everywhere, and, nourishing life, it reminds the speaker of Mary. The conceit is developed as he declares that, first, by praying for men Mary mediates between them and God: sharing men's human feelings as a mother would, she graciously intervenes so that grace may be given to men's hearts to make them Christlike—so that Christ can constantly be re-conceived and re-born and every place on earth can be a new Nazareth or Bethlehem. In these effects, she is everywhere, mothering and nourishing like the air. Sec-

[7] And, again, he is above all the poet of incarnation and of the Incarnation. As Father Boyle concludes, "The life-giving power of divine life. . . , the ultimate significance of the Incarnation, is the basic key to all of Hopkins's mature work." See Robert Boyle, S.J., *Metaphor in Hopkins* (Chapel Hill, North Carolina, 1960), p. 195.

ond, blue-robed and mild, she is like the air not only in being the element of interceding grace that sustains men's inner lives, but also in having been the physical element through which God was born as man, through which fire passed into light on earth:

> did air not make
> This bath of blue and slake
> His fire, the sun would shake,
> A blear and blinding ball
> With blackness bound . . .
> So God was god of old.

Because at the Incarnation God's light was filtered through the mild blue of Mary's body, he could be seen in kindly form. And this event is paralleled and signified by the sunlight's being filtered into light, color, life in nature, so that it is partly reproduced by Christlike light's flashing from human beings (who are thus like beacons). The imagery of this poem, then, includes and relates the second and third uses of light in "The Deutschland," God as fierce fire and Christ as mild light, made human. Still, the darkness of the world is implied. These lines that begin with the observed phenomenon of air end with a tacit recognition of what man's world is like. They end with a prayerful address to Mary, to be

> my atmosphere;
> My happier world, wherein
> To wend and meet no sin.

Along with passive waiting for grace, action to remove obstacles is required in a sinful, less happy, world: "patience, penance, prayer." The vision is bright. The means to attain it are not easy.

The dappled imagery of light and darkness is, in fact, ubiquitous in Hopkins. For instance, "the fire that breaks from" the windhover relates that creature to the ploughed-down clods that shine and the galled embers that "gash gold-vermillion." It seems clear, however, and important, that the poet can distinguish several sorts of light: the light of earthly nature, as in "God's Grandeur," which turns to darkness as it dies; the light of mortal human selves, as in "To What Serves Mortal Beauty?" which becomes dark only insofar as it is mortal and removed from a divine source; the light of God himself, the flame of the Father in "The Deutschland" that makes use of deadly darkness to evoke men's own bright inner lights, but also the milder light of the Son, which contends with the darkness in men and which is reflected by those inner lights flashing from the heroic nun and from the windhover.

One question the light imagery in Hopkins' poetry might be taken to pose is whether these several sorts of light form an imaginative pattern, whether they are related accidentally or essentially. We have seen that Hopkins, like other Victorian poets, both appreciates the beauty of natural light and recognizes its harshness. This can be a matter of mood. He can alternately derive hope and joy from daylight, as Tennyson does from the dawn in "The Two Voices," and see it as bafflingly irrelevant to his own inner darkness, as Tennyson does in the early lyrics of *In Memoriam*, where the dawn is "blank." He can recognize the ambiguity of nature's light, its significance depending upon mood and point of view—as Tennyson perhaps does in "The Vision of Sin," which ends, "God made himself an awful rose of dawn," and as Arnold does in "The New Sirens" and Swinburne in "The Lake of Gaube," for examples. But Hopkins' thought is more systematic, being founded on dogma, than that of most other Victorian writers, and for him a proper response to the light of nature must distinguish it from but also specifically relate it to the fire which is human inscape—and to God the "Orion above." The problem is one of personal belief but also one of poetic imagery.

Victorian imaginations, still largely dominated by the grandeur and the difficulties of the Romantic temper, repeatedly brood upon the relation of man to external nature, of the human figure to the landscape. In Hopkins' scheme of imagery, this becomes specifically the problem of how the light of self, the flash of human inscape, is related to the natural lights and beauties of the world. Hopkins' answer can be given only by reference to the light of God in Christ. A relationship is definitely established in "That Nature is a Heraclitean Fire and of the Comfort of the Resurrection," the poem whose title both states a proposition and introduces a subject for contemplation. Joining the proposition about nature constantly inconstant and the contemplation of the fact of an unnatural or miraculous event breaking into the otherwise continuous natural flux, the poet can observe the supposed nature of men and assert the true state of mankind.

Like so many other lyrics about natural loveliness, this poem begins with a literal description of a scene. And, again characteristically, the poet is attracted by the sky and light effects. Clouds are like puff-balls, or pillows, or groups of roisterers thronging the heavens, gleaming "in marches." They sparkle as they march or move along, or they brighten up large areas, territories in the sky. Bright rays of sun make strips of light (shives, which are slices or threads) and ropes of shadow (if "tackle" means rope) under the arches of elm trees. The light and shadow produce stripes, lacy patterns with lances or lashes of brightness on the ground, and when the bright and dark "pair," the landscape is literally seen as pied or dappled, as spotted. For the moment this seems like a delightful dappling, as it has been in "God's Grandeur." Still, the evidence is that storms occur in this world: yesterday's tempest has left some marks. And, precisely as in "God's Grandeur," man's treading down and marking natural beauty also flaws it—even though ministering winds erase the marks as natural grandeur renews itself.

Delightfully the bright wind boisterous ropes, wrestles,
                                              beats
    earth bare

Of yestertempest's creases; in pool and rutpeel parches
Squandering ooze to squeezed dough, crust, dust; stanches,
  starches
Squadroned masks and manmarks treadmire toil there
Footfretted in it.

The boisterous wind moves in a current across the
ground as if it were a rope pulled rapidly; in swaying
things here and there it seems to be wrestling, and even
to be beating against the earth in its playfulness, as it
blows away or flattens out the litter left by yesterday's
rain storm. The wind and sun dry up, or parch, into
dusty peels the mud of pool and ditch (rut), making
the ooze spend or squander its wetness and become
damp earth like dough that can be kneaded—and, at
last, become crisp dry dough, or crust, hard earth with
a residue of dust. In fact, the wind appears not only to
stanch wetness, as one would stop up a wound and dry
it, but also, like an efficient servant, to starch and leave
both clean and crisp the rumpled earth's very "masks
and manmarks," those signs of human habitation that
cover up the landscape. These are the artificially ar-
ranged (squadroned) signs of man's pedestrian toil on
the boggy earth. "Treadmire toil" suggests also the
futility of most human labor, the sense of man's being
"bogged down." Man has "footfretted [marks] in it,"
has disturbed the earth, just as his tramping over any
creature might "fret" it. The first sentence of the poem,
then, four lines long, describes the sheer delight of sky,
light, and earth. The second, just over four lines long,

again shows nature renewing itself after man has marred its beauty. The third sentence, marking the end of a primary stage in the poem, sums up these meanings and implies much more, using the imagery of fire from the ancient philosopher Heraclitus: "Million-fueled, nature's bonfire burns on." In spite of men, it would seem now, the world of lovely things continues to exist. But even more than the clouds, the sunlight and the parching, starching wind do, all of them images that hint of change, the philosopher's image of the bonfire poses difficulties. All things are burning, Heraclitus said, and constant change is the only reality. Fire has to feed on fuel that cannot literally, like the mythical phoenix, renew itself; so the fire of nature is constantly renewed only as the millions of inscaped, individual, parts of nature are constantly consumed and utterly destroyed. The life of nature, then, means the endless death of all its parts. And, after all, like the elm tree and its leaves, the body of man is a part of nature, one of the fuels in its burning. For all the delight of this first stage and for all the excitement of the phrase, "nature's bonfire burns on," there is an uneasy undertone heard in the qualifying words, "million-fueled."

Even so, the first nine lines of the poem are mainly a celebration of natural vitality. Appropriately, the second stage is introduced as a contrast. For once, Hopkins marks his transition with the adversative, "but." If the "Heraclitean Fire" begins as a nature poem comparable with "God's Grandeur" and "Pied Beauty," it proceeds as a reflection on man's mortality, and thus becomes rather like "Spring and Fall." It proceeds in sober, clear, and shorter sentences, with little of the playful echoing and verbal delight of the first section, where the poet has teased, tricked, skipped, and poured out his joy until he and his reader are breathless; and he has in fact written in "gay-gangs" of words, repeating sounds constantly in alliteration and internal rhyme just as the very life of bonfire nature repeats, sustains, always varies and yet constantly restates itself. Now, instead, the words move heavily. "Both are in an unfathomable, all is in an enormous dark / Drowned." And Hopkins' imagery, rather than one of skies and brightness, is one of light quenched, darkness, drowning, blurring, and emptiness. For now his subject is not aesthetic but moral, and the point of view is not the artist's so much as the mortal realist's. Once more the idea of inscape, of unique selfhood, provides for this shift. Seen only as a part of nature, man has the most fully developed individual identity in the landscape. And so, even if he litters and frets the rest of nature with his trash, with his marks, he himself is the finest mortal thing in a world of mortal things, the pride of all nature.

But quench her bonniest, dearest to her, her clearest-selved
    spark
Man, how fast his firedint, his mark on mind, is gone!

Man's mortal spark, his bodily beauty and natural grace, can be quenched by water, by tempest and wrecking, or merely by burning itself out. One way or another, it dies. And this fact is no less painful to Hopkins than it is to the Tennyson of *In Memoriam*. Now clearly, man's mark on mind is as dear as his mark on nature can be fretting: this "firedint" mark is his communicating of self to other selves, other minds. But, as "The Lantern Out of Doors" has put it, the bright mark of self is soon consumed by death or distance, as individual men soon die and are forgotten. The mortal brevity of nature's highest form makes both the form and all of nature seem now dark and melancholy:

Both are in an unfathomable, all is in an enormous dark
Drowned. O pity and indignation! Manshape, that shone
Sheer off, disseveral, a star, death blots black out; nor mark
    Is any of him at all so stark
But vastness blurs and time beats level.

Again darkness and drowning are opposed to light and vitality. But now manshape is merged into landshape, or landscape, and all is darkened, all is dead, all shape is lost. For Hopkins, life is defined by individual shape, by inscape, the unique shape naturally evolving from an inner principle of being that is precisely "disseveral" because it is one, not several, not general or typical. Like his much admired Duns Scotus, with his individuating principle of *haecceitas*, or concrete separate being, Hopkins can conceive of universal nature only as existing in shapes. Ironically, however, the very constancy and self-renewing of nature that the first stage of this poem celebrates—the fact that "nature is never spent"—is what has to destroy all forms, just as, biologically, birth has to imply death. Time "beats level" the very mark or memory of any man just as today's wind "beats earth bare" and stanches "manmark." What the speaker now sees is what he saw at first, but he sees with different eyes, from a different vantage point, or, one might say, in a different season of the mind, the season not of spring morning but of fall evening. He sees that life in space and time must mean, for men as well as for everything else, death in space and time. Seeing this, he imagines all space and time not as a bonfire really but as a shapeless, chaotic, great ocean of darkness: "Unfathomable," "enormous," vast.

The adverb "delightfully" gives a key to the first stage, the phrase "pity and indignation" sets the mood of the second, and the verb "to be" defines the sense of the third and final stage, the resolution. This begins "Enough!" The exclamation can be taken in the usual sense, "Enough of all this morbid reflection," meaning that it is nonsense or wrong to dwell on such melancholy thoughts. In fact, however, and the point is relevant to Hopkins' dark "terrible sonnets" of his very late period (this poem is, of course, one of his last), it can better be read to mean no more than what it literally says. The reflections on mortality have gone on not too long but simply long enough. It is good and necessary to think, even in pity and indignation, of how natural beings die, but one can dwell on such matters only so long. The first and second stages are both necessary to lead one on to the final stage. And this final reflection on what it means for man truly to *be* represents a higher version of the subject with which the poem began. For the subject now again is renewal, the renewal of life. First, nature renews itself after storms and pollutions. Second, since nature is like a great fire, in renewing itself it destroys all its individual forms; and from man's point of view this fact makes all of nature dark and terrible because within it shape, or specific being, is ephemeral. But, third, a man's shape or being can be renewed as a fire is, and yet not destroyed, because it is more than natural. In nature's renewal of its fire there can be no resurrection, for nature consumes shape; the supernatural renewal restores and preserves shape, for it is precisely a resurrection of the body. So "the Resurrection" of Christ, which sets the pattern for an ultimate resurrection of all men's bodies, is a "heart's clarion" like the trumpet call of the angel Gabriel on the last day.

> Away grief's gasping, joyless days, de-
>   jection.
> Across my foundering deck shone
> A beacon, an eternal beam. Flesh fade, and mortal trash
> Fall to the residuary worm; world's wildfire leave but ash:
>   In a flash, at a trumpet crash,
> I am all at once what Christ is, since he was what I am, and
> This Jack, joke, poor potsherd, patch, matchwood,
>   immortal
>   diamond,
>   Is immortal diamond.

"Grief's gasping," the dejection of "joyless days," is what the darkest poems about the sense of self have expressed. But now, in this great and almost final poem, the imagery is echoed, and the themes are more succinctly developed, of Hopkins' most ambitious earlier work, "The Deutschland." Here again the "foundering deck" means not only tempest and wreck but also the setting in which a beacon can shine. The heroine of "The Deutschland" is herself described as a "blown beacon of light," but both poems suggest that man's light reflects Christ's, responding to or flashing back his flame. And in this final mood the poet is willing to let time and space blur, to let the flesh fade, the mortal body be consumed by worms and by the Heraclitean fire that leaves only ash, the literal dust to which mortal bodies return. For the flash of light reveals an inner shape that outlasts infinitely the splendid but brief natural form. A man, for Hopkins, is like the windhover and any other creature that reveals Christ's inscape, and yet he is much more than any other creature can be: he is what Christ is "in a flash." He is Christ-like when he flashes forth his own light all of a sudden. And he is what Christ is "at a trumpet crash," at the clarion call signalling the resurrection of all bodies on the day of judgment. The tenses—what Christ was on earth, what I am, what bodies will be at last—are all merged in an eternal present, a being essentially out of time. "I am," this body "is." Time is still kept in mind, as Christ "was what I am," a man incarnate in the flesh, at a point in history, but the meaning of all human history since that time—and "since" means both "because" and "ever since"—is eternal as well. Everything in time belongs partly to nature, but what is wholly natural is fuel in the temporal bonfire. Man exists not only in time, as Christ has been not only of the mortal flesh. Thus, a man, who appears to be and partly is common, "Jack" the common man, and trivial, a "joke," who appears to be mere clay, "potsherd," and fuel for the all-consuming fire of time, "matchwood," is really more than all this. Hopkins has used the term "Jack" several times before: in "The Candle Indoors," in the lines (about "Jackself") "My own heart let me have more pity on," and in the fragment that begins, "The shepherd's brow, fronting forked lightning," in which "Man Jack the man is, just." In each place the name suggests an everyman, a common and a dull sort of creature. In the "Heraclitean Fire" Jack the ordinary self becomes a diamond. This last image carries the sense of infinite durability, for a diamond is the hardest of substances and is indestructible by fire. It also suggests the beauty of form that has been produced by stress, as the carbon of the jewel is like the earth and ember of "The Wind-hover," flashing forth its brilliance only after having been submitted to intense pressure. And the diamond, for all its brilliance, is not so much the source as the reflector of light, catching it and flashing back. The immortal diamond is the creature and not the creator, even though at best it imitates and beautifully shows forth the divine and perfect light.

The "Heraclitean Fire" calls for such explication as

this not because of its ambiguous phrasing and syntax, for it is less ambiguous than "The Windhover" and much of "The Deutschland;" and in fact the first part, its verbally most difficult one, has a total meaning extremely simple and obvious. Rather, the best of Hopkins' verse sustains a thinking-out of one's response to it, as the last part of this poem does, because for him art and thought are one. The rhyme, rhythm, and imagery *are* meaning, and it is as important in reading Hopkins to observe the ironic rhyming of "spark" and "dark," the change in speed of the sentences, from "all is in an enormous dark" to "a heart's clarion!" and the several implications of "dust," "bonfire," and "diamond," as it is to know the eschatology of the resurrection of the body.

In his thinking and feeling through images, often ambivalently, Hopkins is, again, as recognizably Victorian as Tennyson or Arnold. The difference is that his ambivalence is emotional but not, so to speak, intellectual; at best, his images both invite a double response and retain a single meaning. Men's inscapes are expressed in the observed lights of nature, as they are natural and mortal; yet the light that shapes an individual being is the reflection as well of divine light. And the image, of the body, the beacon, or the diamond, remains one. This is why, in spite of all his sufferings and anxieties—and he is quite as much in earnest about man's life, the beauty of nature, and the will of God as any other Victorian—Hopkins seems to have a more consistent imagination, in dealing with the largest of themes, than many of his contemporaries. The danger of this consistency might be his striking the reader as narrow, as repetitive. Still, his imagery is specific and real, and his traditional response to Victorian questions about man and nature is as rich, complex, and personal as it is essentially paradoxical. He is more technically original and not much more limited by subject than George Herbert. Like Herbert and unlike the Tennyson of the *Idylls*, who is also deeply concerned with spiritual self and physical nature, Hopkins has full intellectual control of his imagery and plot. For Tennyson's attempted image of Christ, a King representing pure spirit in conflict with the senses, is actually a Manichean anti-Christ who can only demonstrate how sterility and death, not marriage and its promise of birth, result from this conflict.[8] If Hopkins' intellectual control of image and action is more consistent than Tennyson's, his point of view toward self and nature —as distinct from mood—is more consistent than, for instance, Arnold's; in Arnold's poetry, the ocean of external nature is sometimes man's exemplar of natural virtue and sometimes wholly alien to man. And al-

[8] For the failure of Arthur's marriage in *The Idylls of the King*—reflecting a divorce of "sense" and "soul"—see "The Theme of Marriage in Tennyson," *The Victorian Newsletter,* XII (1957), 6–10.

though it is not necessarily a fault when a poet shifts the sense of a metaphor or symbol from poem to poem— with certain writers, one might argue, the result is freshness and variety—Arnold's shifting reveals an uncertainty about how to define or imagine man and nature, an uncertainty that makes the tone in his straightforward intellectual poems ring false by sounding either shrill or vague, as Hopkins' poetic statements of belief —even those that are relatively flat—virtually never do. Finally, Hopkins sustains his imagery within a poem much more consistently than Swinburne can, with his kaleidoscopic images of praise for freedom from all dogma and imposed forms. Tennyson writes poetry with more profoundly mysterious and more powerful symbolism; Arnold has a greater range and variety of mythic sources and ideas; and Browning has more dramatic force, more negative capability. Yet, compared with his major contemporaries, with whom he shares so many interests, Hopkins is more often able to concentrate into the brief lyric a clearly conceived, a coherently imagined, "philosophic" meaning. This is so because, as the consistency of his descriptive and metaphoric language from poem to poem may suggest, he maintains a central and single, if complex, idea of man and nature.

Not that Hopkins is in every respect superior to other Victorian poets. But within his range and at his best, his artist's imagination orders idea, plot, iconography, and tone in a way quite remarkable for his period, while using the themes of his period. Such poems, both personal and intellective or "objective," as "The Windhover," "Spring and Fall," and, especially, "That Nature is a Heraclitean Fire" are as luminous, as clear and whole, as any of the greatest English lyrics.

6 Hopkins in Our Times

Since 1918, Hopkins has been the subject of a good many critical studies which analyze and often acclaim him.[1] Bridges' own animadversions in his "Preface to Notes" of the 1918 volume have inspired some of the most spirited defenses. And many of the strictures in

[1] Those which appeared before 1949 are very well summed up by Maurice Charney in "A Bibliographical Study of Hopkins Criticism, 1918–1949," *Thought*, XXV (1950), 297–326. The "Conclusion: Desiderata" of this study is especially interesting: "In most need of clarification is Hopkins as a Victorian, seen in terms of the literary, intellectual and historical currents of the later nineteenth century. As a corollary to this, a close study should be made of over-all themes and their expression in the poetry and prose" (p. 319). There are bibliographies of Hopkins criticism also in *Immortal Diamond: Studies in Gerard Manley Hopkins*, ed. Norman Weyand (London, 1949) and in Jean-Georges Ritz, *Le Poète Gerard Manley Hopkins* (Paris, 1963); John Pick gives a survey of criticism and scholarship in *The Victorian Poets: A Guide to Research*, ed. Frederic E. Faverty (Cambridge, Mass., 1956). A recently published selection edited by Geoffrey Hartman that presents a rich sampling of criticism is *Hopkins* in the Twentieth Century Views series (Englewood Cliffs, N.J., 1966).

that preface deserve to be rejected: for instance,
Bridges' dislike of his friend's "affectation in metaphor," or freshness, of his "perversion of human feeling," or the outright expression of religious feeling, and
of "the naked encounter of sensualism and asceticism,"
a phrase that indicates Bridges' inability to understand
"The Golden Echo" or indeed much religious poetry
from any period.[2] Yet, irritating as the other poet can
be in patronizing Hopkins, he has one or two points to
score. If he is mostly obtuse about "oddity" and "ob-
scurity"—Hopkins has to be odd to mean what he
means, and most of his poetry can be grasped if it is
read aloud and carefully—Bridges does fairly raise the
question of mannerism, of whether omissions of relative
pronouns, for example, do not become more a habit
than an artful means of making sense. He even hints,
without quite making the point, that there is a fault in
poetic ambiguity of the "either-or" kind, when a line
means either one thing or its virtual opposite but cannot
mean both, as distinct from ambiguity of the "both-
and" kind.

Hopkins is neither perfect nor unique. Right as F. R.
Leavis is in his perceptive essay defending the poet
against the obtuseness of his friend and first editor, and
against the normalizing of his verse by Sturge Moore,
Leavis' response to genteel versifiers leads him to set the

---

[2] The phrase certainly applies to Donne and others more
than to Hopkins.

late Victorian Jesuit against the whole of his century in a way that exaggerates his eccentricity and probably overstates the case for his importance as an influence. Hopkins is said to bear "no relation to . . . any nineteenth-century poet," as there is "nothing approaching [his] imagery in subtlety and strength . . . in any other poet of the nineteenth century," and finally he is judged to be "the only influential poet of the Victorian age, and . . . the greatest."[3] To be sure, Leavis is largely concerned in this passage with techniques of rhythm and language in which Hopkins least resembles anyone else anywhere, not with the actually inseparable matters of subject and idea.[4] But there is some technical resemblance of Hopkins to Swinburne, great as the differences are. Hopkins' strong and subtle imagery, mostly drawn from landscape nature, is inspired by the Romantics, especially Wordsworth (perhaps by way of Ruskin) as is the imagery of other Victorian poets. And not only is the influence of Tennyson and Browning on modern poets quite considerable; it is also pervasive in their time, and Tennyson's influence especially is one which Hopkins could not escape, one of which he was aware.

[3] *New Bearings in English Poetry* (London, 1932), pp. 175, 193.

[4] Leavis' citations from Shakespeare are ingenious, but one suspects that carefully selected passages from Browning could stand as equally plausible comparisons with Hopkins—little as Hopkins would like such comparisons.

Leavis was, at any rate, on the side of the angels in 1932, and his dismissal of every other nineteenth-century poet was then less important than his praise of Hopkins. Perhaps, at that moment, an exaggerated claim had to be made if it was to be heeded at all. We may now be closer to making a fair estimate of Hopkins' place. We may be less in danger than before of reading him as a mere eccentric or an experimenter in poetry. (Both Leavis' use of the term "experiments" and Gardner's well-meant subtitle "A Study in Poetic Idiosyncrasy" seem, in this respect, unfortunate.) We may even have come to realize that he is more than a coterie poet or the poet of the Jesuits.[5] The work of Williams, Richards, Lahey, Gardner, Ritz, Peters, Empson, Daiches, and Pick, among others, should have helped to establish him as a most important Victorian writer.[6]

His poetry should now be allowed to sustain serious critical examination, rather than being apologized for or extravagantly defended as a whole. If there are difficulties now in a serious reader's appreciating this poetry, the difficulties probably have to do not with his prosody but with his psychology, not with his unorthodox technique but with his orthodox faith. And for the

[5] Or, indeed, a versifier whose main interest lies in his prosodic theory and practice.

[6] Conservative as academic anthologists are in such matters, one sign of his being so accepted is the prominence given Hopkins by the Faverty *Guide to Research* on Victorian poets.

non-religious reader who can grasp and enjoy Herbert, Donne, or Milton, these need not be too great.[7]

They need not be more, at the most, than grounds for qualifying judgment. We are no longer likely to write or read unqualified judgments of Hopkins: such a sweeping condemnation as Yvor Winters', asserting that the poet expresses overwrought emotion instead of making lucid statements about human experience, sounds as odd as Leavis' praise might have sounded twenty-five years before it.[8] But Geoffrey Hartman's recent essay, suggesting that, in comparison with Browning or Crashaw, Hopkins seems narrow, poses a real question.[9] It is the question whether Hopkins' range of experience and thought is not so small as to limit sharply his importance. The poet whose moods are contemplation, ecstasy, and spiritual dryness, whose

[7] But a non- or anti-religious set of mind has accounted for some sympathetic misunderstandings, especially the idea that there was an inner conflict between the priest and the poet in Hopkins.

[8] The Winters essay, "The Poetry of Gerard Manley Hopkins," is in *The Function of Criticism* (London, 1957), pp. 103–156.

[9] In his 1966 collection of essays on Hopkins this is the one new piece of criticism ("Introduction: Poetry and Justification," pp. 1–15). The comparison with Browning is unusual, but Hopkins has often been written of as being in the tradition of Crashaw. Yet one is tempted to agree flatly with Elsie Phare upon this matter (if not on many others) when she comments that "the points at which Hopkins resembles Crashaw are apt to be his weakest." See *The Poetry of Gerard Manley Hopkins* (Cambridge, 1933), p. 13.

subjects are natural beauty and supernatural grace, both strictly defined, lacks the dramatic vigor, the ironic humor, and the earthly passions, the sense of moral indignation and the sense of honest and despairing doubt that mark much of nineteenth- and twentieth-century art.

We have had to admit that Tennyson has a much greater range of techniques and styles, that Browning has more variety of setting, tone, and speaker, that even Arnold ranges farther philosophically than Hopkins. His small production of verse, too, raises the problem of how Hopkins is to be considered among the poets. We may not accept Gardner's argument for his being "major"—certainly not if the category of major English poets is limited to six or eight names—or agree with Leavis' judgment that he is the "greatest" English poet of the nineteenth century.[10] Yet, and without playing the parlor game of listing and ordering the major or the great in literature, we can surely now assert that Gerard Manley Hopkins is one of the enduring geniuses of his age, that his art is as intense as it is narrow or concentrated, and in fact that within his apparent limitations of mood and subject he expresses or implies several of the most important attitudes and objects of Romantic and of post-Romantic art.

[10] Gardner, however, accepts both Swinburne and D. G. Rossetti as major poets; in his sense of the term it undoubtedly applies to Hopkins. See, in the second volume of Gardner's study, *Gerard Manley Hopkins* (London, 1958), the "Epilogue: Major or Minor?" pp. 368–78.

For the great preoccupations of modern writers remain those defined by Romanticism. These are not so much questions of theology, ethics, or social relations as they are questions about the self, of how a man is to define and regard his identity, and about the relation of the self to the order or disorder of nature. And these are Hopkins' preoccupations. In the poems we have looked at closely he is concerned specifically with the images of creatures seen within a landscape, and above all with the place of human inscape, the most distinct shape of self, in the whole shape of creation. He sees physical nature as opposed to and as parallel with human nature, as engulfing the mortal self, inspiring the immortal self, expressing human mortality, and being transcended by human immortality. His several ways of relating the human being to the landscape may deny the Romantic impulse to merge subject and object. His nervous self-consciousness and ambivalent response to natural images may be Victorian rather than modern, in contrast with later poets' defiant existentialism and bleak acceptance of an indifferent physical universe. But he is always concerned, as are Wordsworth, Coleridge, Tennyson, Hardy, and Eliot, with the human figure in the natural world.

Hopkins perceives that the relations between self and nature are complex, that they seem to vary. The world outside can be the world of tempests, buffeting man and proving the weakness of his inscape as well as proving the strength of his soul. This is the hard seascape world of "The Deutschland." It can also represent, can

shadow forth in its own nature, the higher Christlike
nature of man, as the buffeting wind and the bird do in
"The Windhover." At the same time, landscape nature
represents in its ephemeral forms the parallel fragility
and brevity of human shapes, of the wholly natural self,
as it does in "Spring and Fall." Finally, the world's
bonfire nature, which provides both stress and a source
of knowledge and which, being both parabolically and
physically like human nature, affects man directly, is
given to be accepted and understood but also to be
transcended. This is the sense of the "Heraclitean Fire."
There is complex consistency in Hopkins' imagination,
for this final sense is implicit in the earlier poems. And,
for the reader who cares to translate a poet's language
into the language of his own experience, it may be a
sense that is not limited to theology. Of course the
poetry of Hopkins is almost all religious and is based on
dogma. Its meaning, however, is as general and as psy-
chologically valid, as it is dogmatic. We can fairly para-
phrase to say Hopkins believes that the universe which
a man lives in both threatens and teaches him, and that a
man's personal value transcends the value of any objects
in that universe; for whether or not he calls himself
immortal, the meaning of his life outlasts his death.

Grasping the joy, the suffering, and the affirmation
that Hopkins communicates in his art does not necessarily mean accepting his faith. The faith has no doubt
helped him, in any case, to achieve an art often more
lucid and consistent, often more rich and more intense,

than that of his comparable contemporaries. But, Catholic and Victorian, he is still a strikingly individual voice expressing his own inscape and repeating no other's song. Hopkins is very much of his age in being self-conscious while he affirms the self, in being conscious of alienation from external nature while he compares and metaphorically identifies man and nature; but he is of his age, too, in being intentionally and peculiarly himself, with a style as unmistakably his own as Carlyle's, or Browning's, or Swinburne's. By declaring "myself I speak," he agrees with the Romantic (and Victorian) theory of art, and he declares himself a man of his century. In the latter half of this century he can be read and understood, surely, as one of the most impressive of that century's poets.

Index